DUMB POLITICS

THE POLITICAL RHETORIC AND
BLISSFUL IGNORANCE OF A GENERATION

DUMB POLITICS

THE POLITICAL RHETORIC AND
BLISSFUL IGNORANCE OF A GENERATION

TANNER T. ROBERTS

DEFIANCE PRESS
& PUBLISHING

Dumb Politics: The Political Rhetoric and Blissful Ignorance of a Generation

ISBN-13: 978-1-940835-21-7 (Hard Cover)
ISBN-13: 978-1-948035-24-8 (Paperback)
ISBN-13: 978-1-948035-22-4 (eBook)

Library of Congress Control Number: 2018911262

Published by Defiance Press and Publishing, LLC

Bulk orders of this book may be obtained by contacting Defiance Press and Publishing, LLC at: www.defiancepress.com.

Public Relations Dept. – Defiance Press & Publishing, LLC
281-581-9300
pr@defiancepress.com

Defiance Press & Publishing, LLC
281-581-9300
info@defiancepress.com

To Aliza. You are the motivation and inspiration behind everything I do to make myself better.

TABLE OF CONTENTS

Table of Contents

Chapter 1—Dumb Politics

On April 7, 2018, the official Twitter of the Women's March tweeted, "The shutting down of Backpage is an absolute crisis for sex workers who rely on the site to safely get in touch with clients. Sex workers' rights are women's rights."[1] The Women's March organization is a left-wing group whose aim, according to its website, is to "create a society in which women—including black women; native women; poor women; immigrant women; disabled women; Muslim women; [and] lesbian, queer, and trans women—are free and able to care for and nurture their families, however they are formed, in safe and healthy environments free from structural impediments." In addition to promoting other left-wing causes, the Women's March advocates that "women deserve to live full and healthy lives, free of all forms of violence against our bodies."

So now that the almighty righteousness of the Women's March has been established, it is important to look at its defense of Backpage—the former website www.backpage.com. Backpage was an online forum designed to provide local classifieds—but which mostly served as an outlet for prostitution. The law eventually caught up with Backpage, and an investigation revealed that some of the prostitution ads on the website included minors as young as fourteen, as well as other women who had been forced into sex trafficking. Yes, that's right, the Women's March—champion of all women's rights—described the shutting down of Backpage as a "crisis." The active abuse and exploitation of women lost one of its greatest outlets, and America gained a serious calamity on its hands. Not only is it a crisis, according to the Women's March, but it is also infringing on sex workers' rights. The March made this claim as if completely oblivious to the fact that sex workers gave up their "workers' rights" when they began working in an illegal profession. It is comparable to advocating against the unlawful seizure of drugs from drug dealers because they have now lost potential profit on their supply. Drug dealers, much like prostitutes, don't have the same workers' rights and have committed the worst crime of all against the federal government: income tax evasion. The Women's March is the epitome of what I call "dumb politics."

Dumb politics is that act of promoting policies and ideas that subsidize groups at the expense of others. It ignores the negative laws of unintended consequences and the third-party outcomes, it becomes hypocritical in equity and equality, it uses emotional responses over rational analysis, and it uses derogatory vernacular to promote class and social warfare. Although the Women's March founders' reasoning may be rooted in the best intentions, it operates under an umbrella of inclusiveness that conflicts with the very mission it is trying to achieve. Its cause is hypocritical, its message is ironic, and its stance wavers constantly.

Dumb politics can spread from one generation and completely metastasize into the next. Ask any "woke" (a term once used to refer to awareness of systemic racism that has now been transformed to define one's self-perceived intellectual superiority in politics and social justice) millennial what special interest group in Washington is responsible for the alarming death toll in the United States, and the answer would probably be the National Rifle Association (NRA). Never mind the hundreds of thousands of deaths Planned Parenthood is directly responsible for each year at the taxpayers' expense. Even late-night TV show comedian Jimmy Kimmel said the NRA has the Republican Party's "balls in a money clip."[2] Yet Planned Parenthood has donated nearly the same amount to individual candidates as the NRA since 2012.[3] Jimmy appears to have his balls caught in a dumb politics vise. That kind of testicular snare would make anyone woke.

But recognizing the irony of this scenario requires cognitive thinking. Dumb politics hates cognitive thinking and prefers the naivety of assimilation. By promoting left-wing values, individuals have become less individual and instead conform to those same statist values largely fostered in media, entertainment, culture, big business, and universities. That conformity of thought leads to the reelection of political hacks who exploit the malleable minds of the young and uninformed which, in turn, leads to simply dumb politics. In today's world, it is easy to be a liberal. Generations are becoming more and more susceptible to a herd mentality.

In fact, dumb politics is fostering a generation of high dependency. Consider a study done by the Pew Research Center that found that 33 percent of those 25-29 lived with their parents or grandparents in 2016.[4] Those aged 18-34 living at home surpassed all other living arrangements in 2014 for the first time in more than 130 years. Now, there are many reasons why young people would choose to live with their parents other than being dependent, such as requiring assisted living. However, it is important to point out the standard of acceptable dependency. Millennials receive the worst reputation out of any generation yet, but their parents have advanced this standard of acceptable dependency. This is mirrored in government, where those elected officials, especially the so-called conservatives, continue programs that create perverse incentives that set the standards for incoming representatives. When politicians tell a generation that it is their right to earn $15 an hour without any increase in output, or it is their right to a free education without knowledge of economic consequences, acceptable dependency has been created. One generation fosters the next.

There is a reason why filmmaker and activist Michael Moore wants to lower the voting age to sixteen, a movement that alarmingly has the support of many others. Those at age sixteen are undereducated compared to those at current voting ages, lack real work experience, have little to no fiscal responsibility, and are susceptible to idea conditioning. They comprise the perfect liberal voters Democrats can always count on to vote for them: undereducated, unemployed, irresponsible, and easily influenced. While there are a lot of 16-year-olds who have more of a financial burden and heavier responsibilities that have propelled their experience beyond their years, the majority in the United States do not share those experiences. Not all opinions are created equal. You do not ask 16-year-olds their choice between a traditional 401(k) vs. a Roth IRA. Yet Michael Moore is promoting the idea that the world needs to revolve around those opinions, and those voices should be heard equally. Michael Moore, age 64, is an example of one generation fostering the next. *The New York Times* posted an article titled "Why We Should Lower the Voting Age to 16," in which Professor Laurence Steinberg states:

> The last time the United States lowered the federal voting age was in 1971, when it went from 21 to 18. In that instance, the main motivating force was outrage over the fact that 18-year-

olds could be sent to fight in Vietnam but could not vote. The proposal to lower the voting age to 16 is motivated by today's outrage that those most vulnerable to school shootings have no say in how such atrocities are best prevented. Let's give those young people more than just their voices to make a change.[5]

Using Steinberg's logic, then 15- and even 14-year-old high schoolers should be able to vote because they are susceptible to school violence as well. Laurence Steinberg, age 65, is also an example of one generation fostering the next.

That's exactly how dumb politics spreads. It is the generational nurturing of the idea that everyone's opinion matters and that they are victims of society, not their own self-determination. This is why being critical of obesity and concerned for health has turned into "fat shaming." It is why "involuntary celibacy" (those who want to have sex but cannot find a partner) has somehow become a societal problem, with victims known as "incels" blaming unreasonable standards of sexuality. Yes, this truly is a thing. These people believe they cannot have sex because they are victims of society; thus, we need to redistribute sex. The belief that all inequality is due to victimization is spreading. There is always someone else to blame, whether it is capitalism, white people (irony is lost when all world problems are blamed on white people), racism, or the patriarchy. Richard Edmond Vargas of CNN blames the patriarchy for everything violent in our society in his piece titled, "Guns Alone Don't Kill People, Patriarchy Kills People." Vargas states, "It is no secret, especially these days, that we live in a patriarchal society. Why are we continually surprised when a man takes up arms and commits mass murder?" Vargas goes even further, stating the following:

When I was 19, I followed this script and decided that committing robberies was an acceptable way to deal with the fact that I couldn't pay my rent. Though my girlfriend offered to help me pay it, I saw accepting a woman's help as weakness and decided to rob instead. That led to me being sentenced to 10 years in state prison.[6]

This victimhood mentally helps Vargas escape the realities of his own decision-making. Patriarchy is to blame for him robbing people, not his own idiotic and criminal behavior. Someone else is always to blame. Dumb politics is the way out of accepting responsibility. Vargas goes on to explain how the patriarchy cultivates inherent violence in men. If men are too aggressive to lead, then is it safe to say women are too emotional to lead? Are we truly in a patriarchal society, or have we been moving toward more balanced leadership among genders? Dumb politics says no.

When society is not getting the blame, dumb politics is forcing its values onto those who dare not comply with the liberal agenda. A great example of this force can be seen in what was formerly known as the Boy Scouts. The Boy Scouts was an all-male organization designed to help promote character development and outdoorsmanship, growing boys into young men. However, political correctness took hold of this century-long tradition and forced it to include girls in this patriarchal institution. Dumb politics does not look at the unintended consequences in the face of political correctness. Now the Girl Scouts of America is clamoring for membership, and this female empowerment organization is suffering from those who claim to speak for all women's rights. It is funny how the only group that benefits from this transformation is the male organization, whereas the female organization, which was declining in membership before this change, will be the one that suffers most. Dumb politics does not see the irony. Again, dumb politics' perverse incentives strike again.

Fomenting change just for the sake of change is a dumb politics prerogative. Let's take an institution like the NFL and implement change on the basis of inclusion and diversity. Then try to be honest with yourself about what would happen to the quality of the NFL if it were to force more white players and women onto each team. Is it fair to say that the quality of play would be diminished? Of course, but dumb politics, which promotes equality over all else, even if it makes everyone equally miserable and the institution suffers, would disagree. Intellectual leftists state that their goal is equity over equality in the sense that everyone is given the same chance to succeed. Yet affirmative action hiring is still in place, and college acceptance preference to minorities is still practiced. This puts other races at a disadvantage of opportunity, as merits are based solely on race.

This disadvantage does not apply just to whites. A coalition of more than 60 organizations accused Harvard of holding unreasonably higher standards for Asian-American applicants than other races.[7] How can this be perceived as equity? Equity over equality is not achieved when one group suffers at the expense of another.

With dumb politics, you not only get perverse incentives, but also set an impossible standard of satisfaction. In 2017, Pepsi ran an ad that caused so much backlash that it sparked a response from the company stating: "Pepsi was trying to project a global message of unity, peace and understanding. Clearly, we missed the mark, and we apologize. We did not intend to make light of any serious issue. We are removing the content and halting any further rollout."[8] What was this appalling ad that caused Pepsi to put out such a remorseful statement? The ad was accused of "appropriating" the Black Lives Matter movement when white reality celebrity and model Kendall Jenner hands a Pepsi to a police officer standing in formation at a blockade to a simulated protest march, which prompts happy cheers of celebration when the officer accepts the Pepsi.

It would seem that this commercial had everything needed to satisfy a progressive mindset. A woman in a hijab: check. Ethnic diversity in nearly every single frame: check. Peace signs: check. Marching in protest: check. Transgendered people: check. Homosexuals: check. Oblivious young celebrity using a chance to virtue signal: double check. Some poor dumb soul in that marketing meeting for Pepsi reached deep into his or her bleeding heart for an idea that surely would be invincible to any criticism except from those bigoted right wingers. Unfortunately, they were wrong, and it failed to appease the very demographic it was intended for. The need for dumb politics to appease everyone is an erroneous strategy that typically backfires. If Shaun King, a prominent activist and vanguard to the Black Lives Matter, can lie about being a black man to raise his status in the movement, then who is truly culturally appropriating the cause? But that kind of critical thinking is lost in dumb politics. When Rachel Dolezal, an infamous white woman who thinks she is black, lied about being a black woman to become the president of a local chapter of the National Association for the Advancement of Colored People, dumb politics allowed her to claim race as a "social construct."[9] This kind of behavior is not just an embarrassment; it is a byproduct of a society that nurtures the idea of transforming any idea, sex, or race.

This book is not intended to demoralize or even discredit anyone left of center as being "dumb." Since my own political affiliations are apparent within the first few sentences of this book, I would be remiss if I did not admit that there are highly intelligent liberals out there whose knowledge exceeds the boundaries of politics. Hell, at one point, even Jimmy Carter trained to become a nuclear engineer officer, which takes a considerable amount of intelligence, one would hope. Although a majority of the ideas and issues presented here battle the platforms of social liberalism, it is worth noting that progressivism has advanced some significant strides in civil rights, as well as individual liberties for women. Then again, it has produced some utter failures, such as the Occupy Wall Street movement, which collapsed under its own convoluted message and misdirected efforts.

It is also naive to assume dumb politics applies only to liberalism because plenty of it has been seen within the Republican Party. Although conservatism can be expressed simply by a preference for government taking a limited role in society, Republicans have battled individual freedoms—most predominantly in gay rights. The fight for individualism becomes counterproductive when Republicans allow the government to define what constitutes traditional marriage by using their religious beliefs to limit the freedoms of individuals. Why does the government's role need to be that deep in people's lives? Who are they to deny anyone those rights? It is a dangerous path for conservatives to allow this over-inflated bureaucracy that much control. The argument passes to states' rights, but guess what? State governments are merely smaller extensions of an overbearing bureaucracy that has the power to repudiate individual rights as much as any federal over-reach. This type of hypocrisy certainly falls within the definition of dumb politics.

Freedom can be easily defined as the ability to express ideas and political points unreservedly and without consequences. I certainly would not want to live in a world that prohibits any mindset that differs from my own. The idea is not to dismiss any forms of thought, whether you are a Democrat or a Republican. The ideas promoted by dumb politics are ironic, hypocritical, and contemptible. Dumb politics is Bernie Sanders preaching the importance of multicultural diversity when he represents a state that stands as one of the whitest states in America at 96 percent.[10] Dumb politics is a teenage "activist" wearing a Che Guevara shirt while attending a rally for peace.

Dumb politics is nothing new. Dumb politics comes in cycles of refurbished ideas packaged as protection against ideas that harm the social safe space. Woodrow Wilson (beloved president of the Progressive Era) passed the Sedition Act of 1918 that banned "uttering, printing, writing, or publishing any disloyal, profane, scurrilous, or abusive language about the United States government or the military." Replace the words "United States government" and "military" with *social justice* and *progressive entitlement*, and you have the current censorship from an administered liberal agenda.

One of the major themes discussed throughout this book is the idea and principle of individualism, especially as it relates to collectivism. The idea of individualism is simple; it is the ability as well as the desire to be self-reliant and live life as you see fit to your individual virtues, ideas, judgments, and values. Individualism is what made the founding of our country unique in the sense that we have God-given rights to life, liberty, and the pursuit of happiness with limited government intervention. These rights are preserved for the individual and cannot be interfered with by any other individual or entity. In the pursuit of happiness, it is believed that each individual should retain the product of his or her labors, the idea being that individuals are entitled to what they produce, as opposed to being entitled to the production of others. Self-interest is promoted over the interest of the state, group, and community. With individualism, individuals are free from group norms that bond them to certain ideas based on things such as race, social status, and gender. For example, if an individual is black, he or she has to be a Democrat. If an individual is a hillbilly, he or she has to be a Republican. If an individual is a Philadelphia Eagles fan, he or she has to be a terrible person. Individuals belong to their self-interests, not the conformity of others.

Former slave Frederick Douglass wrote a letter to his ex-master after running away with a fascinating case of individualism.

"I am myself; you are yourself; we are two distinct persons, equal persons. What you are, I am. You are a man, and so am I. God created both, and made us separate beings. I am not by nature bound to you, or you to me. Nature does not make your existence depend upon me, or mine to depend upon yours. I cannot walk upon your legs, or you upon mine. I cannot breathe for you, or you for me; I must breathe for myself, and you for yourself. We are distinct persons, and are each equally provided with faculties necessary to our individual existence. In leaving you, I took nothing but what belonged to me, and in no way lessened your means for obtaining an *honest* living. Your faculties remained yours, and mine became useful to their rightful owner."[11]

Collectivism is the opposite approach. The individual belongs to a community and needs to act accordingly to benefit the welfare of the state over their self-interest. There is no individual gain unless it comes with the benefit of the overall group and individuals must sacrifice themselves to the betterment of that faction. The value of an individual is measured based on the contribution to the group he or she serves. In collectivism, a single identity is established to a collective group rather than an individual. The roots of collectivism are seen in other "isms" such as socialism, fascism, communism, and Marxism.

Melissa Harris-Perry summed up a notion of collectivism while discussing public education during an ad for MSNBC. She stated that:

"We have never invested in public education as much as we should have, because we've always had kind of a private notion of children. Your kid is yours, and totally your responsibility. We haven't had a very collective notion of 'These are our children;' so part of it is that we have to break through our kind of private idea that kids belong to their parents, or kids belong to their families, and recognize that kids belong to whole communities. Once it's everybody's responsibility and not just the household's, then we start making better investments."[12]

This is collectivism believing that a government that cannot properly budget and run a public education system can raise children better than individual parents. Collectivism wants to allow the government the ability to decide what is best for individuals and government.

The criticism of Individualism is the belief that it is entrenched in selfishness. Joe Biden declared that "for too long in this society, we have celebrated unrestrained individualism over common community."[13] Selfishness has no concern for others and typically has gains at the expense of others. But the gains in individualism help a society, economy, and families. When one tries to self-improve and live a life that benefits themselves, it tends to extend to others. Individualism does not rely on collectivism. It does not rely on the prosperity of others to attribute to their individual prosperity.

Dumb politics prefers a collective approach. This helps assimilate groups to believe what they believe. It keeps everyone in line to the established norm.

This book provides chapter-by-chapter analysis of the political rhetoric and blissful ignorance that has taken hold of a generation. The exploits of the left are described in each chapter:

Dumb Name Calling—Dumb name calling looks at the dangerous consequences of loosely using terms such as *racists*, *bigots*, and *fascists*. Those who are astute in dumb name calling typically lack knowledge of the term they are so quick to throw out. These influences have created a tribalism effect where groups are now pitted against each other without having substantial arguments or ideas that make us individuals rather than group-thinking machines.

Dumb Immigration—Seventy-seven percent of lawmakers represent states that do not even share a border with Mexico. U.S. officials have failed the states under Article 4, Section 4 of the U.S. Constitution in regard to the safekeeping of our own country. Border security has shifted from a constitutional protection to a humanitarian crisis that coincidentally benefits one party. This chapter focuses on how the left has exploited this crisis and all the issues associated with a loosely secured border.

Dumb Economics—Dumb economics ignores the rules of unintended consequences in favor of moral objectives. Achieving equality has replaced the fundamentals of achieving success. The "Dumb Economics" chapter focuses on the blissful ignorance politicians exploit in concepts of wages, employment, taxes, income, and productivity.

Dumb Education—Ideology imposition institutions have outlived their purpose of furthering higher education. Instead, diversity of student population is given priority over diversity of thought. The "Dumb Education" chapter takes a deeper look into the assimilation of group thought in education as well as the declining benefits of a college education.

Dumb Culture—There is no debating the fact that conservatives have lost the cultural war. This chapter examines the ideologies of the left that are pushed on the biggest platforms such as music, movies, sports, and entertainment. These agendas are implanted in the young and continue to condition our mindsets. Although the landscape may be too far gone to alter, those who do not conform to these principles can still battle dumb culture to minimize its effect on future generations.

The purpose of this book is to point out the long-term effects that are detrimental to my generation, the generation after, and the generation before mine. Dumb politics does not have a time frame, but it has been emerging in recent times to a substantial level of near idiotic politics. Truth bears no meaning in the comfort of feelings and opinions.

CHAPTER 2—DUMB NAME CALLING

It is important to cover this topic first because dumb name calling spreads through many of the other topics.

Political name calling detracts from sensible political discussion. You might say, "Well, your book cover has the words 'dumb' and 'ignorant' in it; stop being a hypocrite." While that may be true, here is the difference: political name calling has become more viable as an attempt to discredit someone's affiliations by labeling them with either "extreme" or "hateful," or sometimes both, delineations. A less extreme example would be calling Democrats socialists just because they are Democrats. The assumption is that Democrats want more economic distributive policies and higher taxes on the rich. That does not make them socialists, as we have seen capitalist markets with high tax rates and larger social benefits. It is not that they are socialists; rather, it is that they promote policies that inhibit growth and productivity through those policies. That is a very simple example. There are plenty of Democrats that would proudly boast about being socialists. There are not many conservatives that would boast about being fascists or racists, as they are commonly labeled.

But name calling redirects the political conversation. The goal is to trigger the other side to a point where getting the biggest reaction is more valuable than getting the best possible point of view across. It is kids in the playground calling each other names they've learned, yet don't know what their actual meanings are. Name calling has the worst unintended (and sometimes intended) consequences on individuals than any topic covered in this book. This can affect people's reputations, their livelihoods, and their personal lives.

Disagreeing with someone is okay. Disagreeing with people and then calling them sexists because they say women are worse drivers than men, is stereotyping, but it is neither productive nor sexist. Saying that women are bad drivers and should be banned from driving is sexist. Can we see the difference? This will be discussed a little more later on.

Dumb name calling provides a foundation for the idea of "provide for a divide." Now I do get that your ideologies can help you frame an idea on whether you are going to get along with someone. For example, I know I am going to disagree and may not be best friends with a liberal who does not watch sports, is vegan, and only drinks craft beer (yes, vegans can drink beer as verified by PETA). There is just not a lot of common ground between us. But respect will still be given to individuals who hold their own convictions, not slander that helps "provide for a divide" among people with conflicting beliefs.

Hillary Clinton brought dumb name calling to a height when she called Trump supporters a "basket of deplorables" at a fundraiser. "You know, to just be grossly generalistic, you could put half of Trump's supporters into what I call the basket of deplorables. Right?" Clinton said. "The racist, sexist, homophobic, xenophobic, Islamaphobic—you name it. And, unfortunately, there are people like that. And he has lifted them up."[1] Name calling from politicians only stirs up the party base and virtue-signals their entire ideology. If they are racist, then we are the party of anti-racism. If they are the party of homophobia, then we are the party of anti-homophobia. Name calling in politics is a ploy to say we are the party of anti-hate, so how can anyone disagree with us? Unfortunately, blissful ignorance falls for their strategies. Not everyone you disagree with has a list of phobias. Not everyone you disagree with is a fascist or Hitler or some other extreme.

FASCISM

According to Madeleine Albright, fascism today is "a more serious threat now than at any time since the end of World War II."[2] Albright would have been just as effective in her fear mongering if she simply stated, "we are all going to die because of Trump." This, of course, is because Trump is a fascist and his fascist supporters put him in power. And it is not just Trump who has been called a fascist. The website Refuse Fascism called Ben Shapiro a "fascist intellectual hitman." Shapiro is an Orthodox Jew who probably would not fare well in fascist Germany of the 1930s. But at least he was called an intellectual, so there is a silver lining. Milo Yiannopoulos has been described as a fascist by many throughout his career. Milo is a homosexual political provocateur who has dressed in drag during a speaking event and he, too, would not fare well in a fascist society, considering that homosexuality does not actually help further a "superior" race, something that is an important part of fascism.

George W. Bush was even called a fascist, most notably by then-MSNBC host Keith Olbermann who, when on the topic of Bush, said, "If you believe in the seamless mutuality of government and big business, come out and say it! There is a dictionary definition, one word that describes that toxic blend. You're a fascist! Get them to print you a tee shirt with fascist on it!... You, sir, have no place in a government of the people, by the people, for the people."[3] Bush was thought of by many on the left as a fascist war criminal. Not even Ronald Reagan could escape being labeled a fascist when Missouri Democratic Representative William Clay stated that Reagan was "trying to replace the Bill of Rights with fascist precepts lifted verbatim from Mein Kampf."[4]

If the word socialist is used too much to describe Democrats, then the same definitely holds true to calling Republicans fascists. What is a fascist? Most definitions are relative and differ, depending on whom you ask. Fascist is no doubt considered a "bad word," a sort of political boogeyman used abusively to describe anyone with differing views, particularly those who are "right wingers." What comes to mind with fascism is racism, dictatorship, Hitler, Nazi, Holocaust, white supremacy, nationalism, etc. You wouldn't be wrong, but you wouldn't be exactly right either.

Most would say that fascism rivals include communism and socialism, though they do have some differences. They are, in fact, derivatives of each other. Throughout history, fascism has become more difficult to define because some of the most famous fascists, such as Benito Mussolini and Adolf Hitler, came about differently. Not only that, but the label is used so broadly that it is nearly impossible to pinpoint a single definition amongst vastly different targets. Progressive-era American muckrakers, known as Progressive Era journalists, praised Mussolini, the first notable fascist, for looking after the little guy and fighting for working class people. Both Hitler and Mussolini were inspired by views of socialists, such as Karl Marx, to limit the effects of the bourgeoisie, individualists and property owners in the middle class, and garner support for government expansion in the name of public interest. One of the main separators of fascism with other "isms" was the institution of "Social Darwinism," which became associated with Nazism and formed into the bad f-word that we know today. Social Darwinism is the distinct difference of fascism from the other "isms" because of its roots in nationality and the belief that the superior race of their country must be preserved. This was the kind of belief that led to the Holocaust and morphed into the fascism we know today, instead of the long-forgotten celebrated Italian fascism of Mussolini during the progressive era.

COMMON FASCIST BELIEFS

- **No individualism**: Everyone works and contributes to the benefit of the state to promote a strong sense of national unity. All needs must contribute to the community first before the individual.

- **Anti-capitalism**: Instead of class socialism, fascists focus more on national socialism that puts the nation first to promote anti-capitalist policies that were meant to benefit the common workers. Private property and ownership existed, but forms of business were more intertwined with government, creating a corporatism structure. In fascism, government controls the means of distribution. Government controls what is best for the people, not what is most profitable for the corpora-tion. A company like McDonalds would not exist because it is not necessary to preserve a society (benefit of the people over profit of the company). Government and business work together to limit competition and guarantee profits for those select companies.

- **State-run education system:** This was to maintain control over the narrative of their messaging.

- **Government takeover of industry and heavy profit sharing:** While some industries remained private, the Nazi party called for the nationalization of all businesses that had been formed into trusts (corporations). In addition, they demanded profit-sharing in large industrial enterprises.

- **Totalitarianism:** Dictatorship, or a single authoritarian figure, is required to control public and private life in the name of benefiting the state.

- **Social Order:** Use of party police to stifle any opposition to the regime. These were the Brownshirts or Storm Troopers that used physical assault methods on any political opponents who threatened their party's platform.

- **Social Darwinism:** Belief that the race of the nation is superior to all other races. Most foreigners and foreign businesses were not given the same rights as those in Nazi Germany who were pure Aryan in race. One of the reasons government controlled the means of distribution was to maintain a superior race of the nation.

Hitler ran on a powerful platform of stronger government, extended benefits, profit-sharing, and anti-capitalist policies that would mark him as a socialist today. However, it was not until Social Darwinism and the focus on nationalism, which spread to Mussolini, that fascism became the slur we know today. A quote such as "more children from the fit, less from the unfit" would sound like something out of Nazi Germany; instead, it is a quote from a heavily celebrated progressive idol named Margaret Sanger, founder of Planned Parenthood. It has been noted time and again that Sanger had a very controversial background, particularly considering she even spoke at KKK rallies on her belief in Social Darwinism.[5]

The term Nazi has been loosely thrown at conservative politicians and their supporters, often without any merit. It devalues an extreme political ideology that really shouldn't be used so carelessly to label *anyone*. The Nazi party had just as many ideologies of the far right as it does the progressive left. In Jonah Goldberg's book, "Liberal Fascism," Goldberg states that "American Progressivism—the moralistic social crusade from which modern liberals proudly claim descent—is in some respects the major source of the fascist ideas applied in Europe by Mussolini and Hitler."

Take a second to learn more about Hitler and his National Socialist German Workers' Party—known as the Nationalsozialistische Deutsche Arbeiterpartei, better known as the Nazi Party—before labeling anyone you disagree with a Nazi. Jump to Hitler's 25-point program (Appendix A, starting on page 159) that helped him and the Nazi Party come into power. Below are some examples from that program that was essentially their creed:

- We demand the nationalization of all trusts (corporations).

- We demand profit-sharing in large industries.

- We demand a generous increase in old-age pensions.

- In order to make it possible for every capable and industrious German to obtain higher education, and thus the opportunity to reach into positions of leadership, the State must assume the responsibility of organizing thoroughly the entire cultural system of the people. The curricula of all educational establishments shall be adapted to practical life. The conception of the State Idea (science of citizenship) must be taught in the schools from the very beginning. We demand that specially talented children of poor parents, whatever their station or occupation, be educated at the expense of the State.

• The State has the duty to help raise the standard of national health by providing maternity welfare centers, by prohibiting juvenile labor, by increasing physical fitness through the introduction of compulsory games and gymnastics, and by the greatest possible encouragement of associations concerned with the physical education of the young.

The conservative party has much less in common with fascism than a social justice warrior would be willing to admit. Dumb name calling is not just slander; it is ignorant and misinformed. You can get into the semantics of communism, Marxism, fascism, socialism, collectivism, Nazism, etc. All those terms are useful to deceive people about the underlying meaning and parallels among them. The fact is that conservative free market principles do not fall in line with a fascist economy. Individualism garners no support in fascism. Why is it that this term is associated with conservatives so much? Because it is considered a derogatory term and is typically associated with racism, as well as a fundamental corporation relationship with government.

A fascist society can exist without an institution of racism. Italy's fascism, led by Mussolini and considered the original fascism, did not have an element of racism or race superiority. Mussolini's fascism was praised by many in America, including Franklin D. Roosevelt. FDR described Mussolini as "admirable" and claims he was "deeply impressed by what he has accomplished."[6] Even progressive writer Roger Shaw described FDR's New Deal plan, which contained some of the social programs we still have today, as a "Fascist means to gain liberal end." Again, if you take out the Social Darwinism of fascism, you might have progressives of today echoing the same support given during the Progressive Era. There are not many millennials that can give you the principles behind fascism today; there are not many people from any generation that can, for that matter. If you were to take Clinton's message and replace it with a fascist principle withholding race preservation, you would have the same support, if not more.

Over the years, there has been an anti-fascist movement, with a network formed called "Antifa" brought on to fight non-existent fascism with fascist techniques. These members dress in black, cover their faces, and use violence at events they deem fascist, such as free speech rallies, college speaking events, and pro-right rallies. Most of these Antifa members are trendy college students, high schoolers, and millennials set out to make a fabricated difference. They are responsible for a lot of the violence done on college campuses.

In 2017, when transsexual Amber Cummings organized a march for anti-Marxism in Berkeley, it was met by violent counter protests from anti-fascist groups wielding weapons and pepper spray. A cringe-worthy video was posted of at least four Antifa members beating a helpless man on the ground with shields, fists, and poles while a group of five others stood idly by, taking pictures and recording videos. Ironically, some of these homemade shields used to beat people had "No Hate" written on them.

Antifa has used pepper spray, Molotov cocktails, and batons to bully those they consider a threat to their ideology. This group has even gone so far as to issue serious threats on social media. Journalist Cassandra Fairbanks was sent a threat by an Arizona Antifa group for the crime of supporting Trump. "Some of us know you very personally cass, and you know how afraid you can really get," a tweet by the group stated. "Be careful doll, for our duaghters [sic] sake." Even after the tweet was forcefully deleted, the individual on the account came back to state, "u better believe we have no prblm threatening our leaders and their kids. Watch ur back alt-reichers. No one's off limits."

Anti-fascist groups are not looking to fight fascism. They are just looking for a fight. They have become the Storm Troopers of the far left. That is what happens when you throw around a term that no one quite understands but symbolizes it with hate and lets that hate fester. Considering that a study done by the Conference on Jewish Material Claims Against Germany, which found that 66 percent of millennials could not even identify what Auschwitz was, it should not be a surprise that they lack proper identification of fascism. In that same study, 22 percent have not even heard of the Holocaust.[7] Perhaps millennial-led groups such as Antifa are not the best representatives to fight the ghost of fascism. It is time for Americans to get off the KKK and Neo-Nazi kick, as those groups have not done anything of significance in years. Innocent bystanders are the ones taking on the violence, not some Klan member.

You probably have heard of the term alt-right or alternative right, especially when it was used heavily during the 2016 election cycle. If the label is not fascist, then it is alt-righter, but the two are mostly used interchangeably. These individuals are less people practicing in society as they are trolling people online for a reaction. Its rise stems from a politically correct culture and combats the social justice warrior mentality. Here is where it is less applicable to just about every conservative commentator that it's been applied to: it has strong nationalist and white nationalist politics. As the Southern Poverty Law Center defines it, "The Alternative Right, commonly known as the "alt-right," is a set of far-right ideologies, groups and individuals whose core belief is that "white identity" is under attack by multicultural forces using "political correctness" and "social justice" to undermine white people and "their" civilization."

The term is said to be brought on by white supremacist Richard Spencer, who runs the National Policy Institute that is "dedicated to the heritage, identity, and future of people of European descent in the United States." Yet the true alt-right, and not those who try to trigger people online, is a small subset of a fringe extremism. But because it is on the right and it is extreme, it has a bright light shining on it that propelled its existence into the national spot light. It is only perceived to be growing larger because more people are being labeled alt-right. Actual growth is a figment of the imagination, but it can appear to be a national crisis. This is a consequence of using terms reserved to a diminutive class. The same effect is seen with fascism and racism. If you start calling everyone fascist, people will start believing, through blissful ignorance, that America is basically Nazi Germany.

DEATH OF STEREOTYPES

Whether you know it or not, we have all stereotyped. It could have been a positive stereotype such as assuming the Asians in your classroom were the smartest, or a negative one such as the dumb, blonde, white girl that likes to drink pumpkin-spiced lattes. But just because we stereotype, it doesn't infer we are racists, sexists, or any other negative connotation. Believing that Asians are smarter than you does not actually fit the definition of racism, which is "a belief that race is the primary determinant of human traits and capacities and that racial differences produce an inherent superiority of a particular race."[8] It is actually doing the opposite. Now, believing a white girl is dumb because of her hair color could be borderline misogynistic or sexist, but it still can be argued that it is a generic stereotype. This is because you are implying that, since she is white and blonde, she is less intelligent than you; therefore, you are superior to her. Yet, even that is a stretch, and most will not link certain stereotypes to their harsher counterparts such as racism and sexism. Or at least they should not. We see stereotypes play out all the time. We see them reaffirmed in movies, TV shows, and commercials. They are used as comedy and entertainment because a lot of stereotypes can hold true to an individual or even a majority, but not as a whole.

Let's just take one of the biggest stereotypes that many people apply. We have all done it—passed someone driving recklessly or slowly and looked into their car window to confirm one of four assumptions: it is an elderly person, a person on his or her phone, a teenager, or maybe even a woman driver. Making these assumptions does not necessarily mean you are sexist. You are not discriminating against women by saying they should not have the right to drive. Nor are you saying that elders, cell phone users, and teenagers should be banned from carrying a license to drive. Yet sometimes these stereotypes have statistical backing. Consider these statistics from the Insurance Institute of Highway Safety (IIHS):

- IIHS concludes that 16- to19-year-olds are three times more likely to crash than drivers over 20.

- Teens are responsible for 12.2 percent of car accidents, while drivers over 65 are responsible for 7.5 percent of accidents.

- Men are more responsible for car accidents; however, they drive a significantly larger number of miles by 40%.

- Men cause 6.1 million accidents per year and women cause 4.1 million.

- Even though there are more women drivers, men drive significantly more miles, meaning women are more of a risk for accidents than men.[9]

Sometimes, stereotypes can confirm your assumptions, but they don't necessarily represent everyone in that category. There are good teenage drivers. There are good elderly drivers. And, of course, there are good women drivers. Just because a noteworthy portion of that said group fits the stereotype doesn't mean everyone belongs to it. That is where stereotyping can be frustrating to the victim. But does this stereotyping of women drivers make anyone sexist? Does stereotyping elderly and teenagers make you an ageist? The term "ageist/ageism" exists; it is just not as popular as sexism. If someone is going to be labeled a sexist, there needs to be a little more merit than just a simple act of stereotyping. Yeah, it's not very advantageous to assume every woman is a bad driver, but that does not mean we get to devalue the meaning of sexism by calling everyone who may have shared this stereotype a sexist. In today's politically correct dumb name-calling culture, it is easy to forgo a stereotype and jump right to an extreme conclusion. These high sensitivity levels have caused us to walk on eggshells, both digitally and socially.

Gone is stereotyping when it comes to race. Every race is stereotyped. It provides material for comedians and gives people the ability to laugh at themselves once in a while. Hollywood and the entertainment industry love stereotypes because they can provide a quick and easy laugh from an audience. However, people can come off as being "racially insensitive," especially when they go after certain stereotypes. Racially insensitive, not racist. If a white person said, "There is no way I'm going into that neighborhood; I don't want to be shot," about a predominantly black neighborhood in the ghettos, that may be racially insensitive, but what it's not is racism. If that same white person said, "There is no way I'm going into that neighborhood; I hate black people," then there is a clear-cut case of racism.

Stereotypes can be racially insensitive, but they are not always racist. There are negative and positive stereotypes for all races. For every great black athlete, there is a "white man that can't jump." We cannot set a hierarchy of stereotypes where one group is allowed to use them but the other is not. Conversely, we see this happen when it comes to racism. This is rooted in the term "reverse racism" that essentially says white people cannot be subject to racism the same way other minority groups experience it. So, when journalist Sarah Jeong was hired at the *New York Times* in 2018, and previous Twitter posts were uncovered from her that said such things as "oh man it's kind of sick how much joy I get out of being cruel to old white men" and "Dumbass fucking white people," we are supposed to believe that racism against whites does not exist? When conservative commentator Candace Owens took Sara Jeong's multiple racists tweets like one that stated, "Dumbass fucking white people marking up the internet with their opinions like dogs pissing on fire hydrants" and replaced the word "white" with "black" and "Jewish," Owens was the one who received a ban on Twitter for "Rule Violation." Owens is a black conservative who simply substituted another race word in place of the race that was being targeted in Sara Jeong's multiple hate tweets. Yet Owens was the only one banned. Even Twitter has a double standard when it comes to racism against whites versus racism against all other races.

The belief is that the core of racism is rooted in the systematic oppression of a minority group at the benefit of a dominant race. This is a mainstream argument that was even presented on the Netflix show, "Dear White People," when one dialogue argued: "Black people can't be racist. Prejudiced, yes, but not racist. Racism describes a system of disadvantage based on race. Black people can't be racists since we don't benefit from such a system." What exactly do whites have to benefit from being racist? How is it justified that one race can make comments that link a race to being inferior, yet it is not considered racist because that inferior race is a majority? Race superiority does not fall under a simple stereotype nor is it simply considered racially insensitive. One can argue that stereotyping leads to racism or other "isms." The counter argument is that prejudice, not stereotyping, leads to these types of hate. Prejudiced views come with negative opinions and hostility formed about a particular group or person without any justification. While someone may believe women are bad drivers, it does not mean that person has general negative feelings toward all women. That's why prejudice is more likely to lead to racism than stereotyping. Prejudice is formed from your own negative feelings whereas, with stereotyping, you are just agreeing with what may be an over-assumption about a certain group, even if you feel indifferent.

CONCLUSION

We are to believe that this generation is hyper-aware of issues that are involved in culture and race. What it has morphed into is a culture of dumb name calling because there is no other way for some to combat an idea that conflicts with their own. It is dangerous and very misleading. Terms such as racist and sexist used to have actual meaning. With that belief, now anyone wearing a "Make America Great Again" cap can be labeled racist, sexist, or fascist, never mind the other terms such as bigot and the phobias that go along with them.

When men get blamed for creating some kind of social construct on the standards of beauty for women, they are left wondering who created standards for the beauty of men. But that is how the patriarchy, one of the favorite terms of a generation, works. This is another oppression claim—this time in the form of male oppression. Yet more women have jobs, get equal pay for equal work, are attending college more, performing better in grade school, and are jailed less than men.

Attacking political opponents through slander and libel only fuels the growing battle over dumb name calling. It is a key component when it comes to the term, "provide for a divide." It is simply the idea that people or institutions are actively pitting us against each other by creating negative connotations about a particular group before a conversation can even start.

CHAPTER 3—DUMB IMMIGRATION

If you have not heard, we are a nation of immigrants. That is almost the prerequisite statement you have to make before every immigration discussion. A lot of Americans are descendants of people who were not born on this land. When I say a lot, I mean just about everyone. This is always a talking point brought up when debating immigration, as if it justifies the means of illegal immigration.

When activist and political organizer Lisa Fithian was asked if Americans should fight for amnesty during a protest for open borders, she replied, "Of course. This is a land of immigrants; it's a land of indigenous people. Immigrants are indigenous people."[1] I would agree with that statement because Americans are immigrants and indigenous. So are Native Americans. So are Mexicans in Mexico. So, who cares? Just because there are immigrants that become indigenous does not grant the right to illegally migrate to a country.

There are economic and security incentives to protect a country's border. All this has become is a virtue-signaling slogan that has been expressed throughout our culture. It is an attempt to instill guilt onto American citizens for the first settlers taking land that did not originally belong to them.

George Mason economist Bryan Caplan asked this simple question on immigration: "What would you think about a law that said that blacks couldn't get a job without the government's permission, or women couldn't get a job without the government's permission, or gays or Christians or anyone else?" This question is posed to make his point, which he states is: "So why, exactly, is it that people who are born on the wrong side of the border have to get government permission just to get a job?" Well, Bryan, why doesn't George Mason University have a 100 percent acceptance rate? Why do people have to seek permission to get into a higher education institute? Isn't it racist, sexist, fascist, and homophobic to list your GPA requirements at 3.0 on your university website? Anyone can make dumb arguments while trying to appear virtuous.

You do not see many people advocating open enrollments in college. It is because it's not feasible; it saturates that university, and essentially makes that university's degree worthless. People go to college, pay tuition, and study hard to get into the top institutions because it is an opportunity for them to earn more throughout their lifetimes. America is much like a university; people have to earn their way into America with merits. One is the land of opportunity; the other is an institution of opportunity.

There was an American Grammy Award-winning band called The White Stripes who came out with a 2007 album with the title song called "Icky Thumb." I have to admit I am a fan of the musicians in that group, but there are lyrics in that song that always remind me of the convictions people hold in dumb immigration. It goes as follows: "White Americans, what? Nothing better to do? Why don't you kick yourself out? You're an immigrant, too." While this may just be a song, there are real life examples of this very thought in everyday exchanges. Take, for example, the heated exchange between Fox 26 Houston's Matt Patrick and the leader of the New Black Panther Party of Houston, Quanell X. After a back-and-forth, Quanell stated his sentiments about Americans, more particularly white Americans, in this statement: "The country belongs to Indians; you white folks stole it from them. You all need to go home; you all need to go back where you came from." Not only that, but Quanell continued on to say, "Let the Indians decide who should pack up and go and I guarantee you black folks will stay and you all will be on the first damn boat leaving here." He finally topped this rant off by saying what a lot of people hold near, dear and true, which is that "white people did not make America and this is not your country."[2] A little bit of racism mixed with group think and topped with ignorance is the delicious recipe for dumb politics in dumb immigration.

So, if it is an opinion held by activists, educators, and culture advocates, it certainly is held by the media. There is an abundance of open border support from outlets such as *Vox*, *The Huffington Post*, *The Washington Post*, *Salon*, and many others. The BBC made a video titled "America is a Stolen Country," which highlights the poverty, alcoholism, and domestic abuse seen on Indian reservations. All points to the fault of Americans. And it is our fault, specifically, the federal government's fault.

In 2016, 8.9 percent of Native Americans were jobless compared to the 4.9 percent for the U.S. as a whole.[3] Native Americans have the highest rate of poverty of any racial group, almost twice the national average. Reservations are typically far from metropolitan areas, limiting the amount of resources and capital for those living in them. The main agencies that oversee Indians on reservations are the Bureau of Indian Affairs and the Bureau of Indian Education, which spend $3 billion per year and have more than 9,000 employees. The government has thrown tons of money into helping improve the conditions on reservations, but it has not worked. A typical solution, done in dumb economics, is to throw more money at something and hope for the best! The government has given Indians land in the form of reservations, but these lands are held in "trust." This means Indians are denied basic property rights to use the land how they want to use it.[4] They are sitting on land that is described as "dead capital" by Nobel Prize-winning economist Hernando de Soto. Indians are prevented from using the land for borrowing against it to raise capital for businesses, they cannot sell it, and they cannot develop on it. Indian reservations have nearly 30 percent of the nation's coal reserves and 50 percent of the potential uranium reserves, as well as 20 percent of known oil and gas reserves.[5] These resources are worth nearly $1.5 trillion. Yet federal control prevents Indians from capitalizing on any natural resources. The same politicians who express that we are a nation of immigrants and try to shame us for being American are the ones keeping Native Americans suppressed.

This truly is a land of immigration. In fact, Native Americans can be considered immigrants as well. Studies through DNA sequences of bones have shown the heritage of Native Americans can be traced back to Siberia and Oceania. Genes have even been linked to native people back to the Middle East and Europe. Timelines conflict on exactly when these groups migrated from Asia to Alaska through the Bering Land Bridge and then to America. The dates range from 13,000-23,000 years ago. Once they arrived, Native Americans split into different groups that created the diversity in genetics and culture seen among different tribes. Indians were certainly native to this land before any European settlement, but they are not Natives, either.

You can say that North American beavers had their land stolen from them. Beavers have fossils here that date back seven million years. But there is no point in arguing ridiculous semantics. It is still important that this land of immigrants certainly includes Native Americans as well. Has the American government always acted in the best interests of Native Americans? Absolutely not, and they continue not to do so in that regard.

Mexico is a land of immigrants as well. Most people associate Cinco de Mayo as being the equivalent of our Independence Day. This is a common misconception. Benito Juarez became the president in 1861 when Mexico was in financial ruin. When Juarez could not pay Mexico's debts, Napoleon-controlled France responded by sending a fleet to storm Veracruz to seize the territory. The Mexican army was able to fight off the French in underdog fashion, despite being vastly outnumbered. The battle lasted from daybreak to early evening on May 5th. Americans tend to celebrate this holiday with more fanfare as an excuse to drink tequila and eat Mexican food. It is celebrated in Mexico but not to the degree at which it is in the U.S.

Mexico has an actual Independence Day and that day is September 16 and is known as the "cry of independence." Their Independence Day has a lot of similarities to how and why the U.S. gained its independence. When Spaniard Hernán Cortés and an army of conquistadors invaded what is now Mexico, they overthrew the native Aztec empire (sound familiar?) and destroyed many native populations with diseases and force (sound even more familiar?). The territory would be called New Spain under the rule of the Spanish regime (sounds very familiar).

After centuries of Spanish rule, a Catholic priest named Miguel Hidalgo y Costilla called for independence and launched a rebellion against the Spanish for the large amounts of taxes going back to Spain, unfair treatment of citizens, and redistribution of land. Much like America, Mexico just wanted out from under the oppressive control of tyrants and to use its ability to form an independent nation. They wanted independence; they fought for it and they got it.

Mexico's foundations are very similar to ours: discovery of new land by foreign invaders that cleared out some of the indigenous populations, who eventually got tired of their rulers, and then fought to form a nation in their image. Try to imagine, if possible, that the reverse was happening in illegal immigration, with American citizens pouring into Mexico. How would that be perceived? In dumb immigration, it might be labeled as another attempt at Manifest Destiny by America.

No one would come to the defense of Americans by saying, "Well, Mexico is a nation of immigrants so they should be more inclusive." It would not happen. It should not happen. There are plenty of countries that got to where they are by immigration and would like to remain the sovereign nation they became. Now things have changed and countries get to decide who comes into these countries. It is what some might even call progressive.

IMMIGRATION IMPOSITIONS

Can you guess what president said this about illegal immigration? "We are a nation of immigrants but we are also a nation of laws. It is wrong and ultimately self-defeating for a nation of immigrants to permit the kind of abuse of our immigration laws we have seen in recent years and we must do more to stop it." Most wouldn't believe it was Democratic President Bill Clinton during his 1995 State of the Union address to Congress or would, at the very least, refuse to acknowledge that a Democrat would ever speak out publicly against the abuse of our immigration laws. Dumb politics today would probably have Bill reverting far from his State of the Union stance on illegal immigration. This position included President Clinton saying that illegal immigrants' use of government assistance continues to "impose burdens on our tax payers." If Mr. Clinton had dared to use this practical rhetoric during Hillary's presidential runs in 2008 and 2016, it would have been more devastating to her campaign than the allegations of rape and misogyny on Bill.

Can you guess what president has deported more illegal immigrants than any other administration up until 2015? Most would make the right guess of President Barack Obama because it was widely reported, due to the hypocrisy shown by those who voted for him. Most would prefer to ignore the fact that Obama deported 2.5 million illegals, more than any other previous administration,[6] but that is what the idea behind dumb immigration has done. It has taken what is considered a sensible approach shared by former liberal presidents and turned it into a partisan assault tool that questions the human nature of those who want to enforce our current border security laws.

The most frustrating belief in dumb immigration is that those who oppose illegal immigration oppose all immigration. Dumb politics only sees closed borders as a humanitarian crisis that leaves innocent people, who only want to pursue a better life, stranded at the border with their kids. This has developed the idea that border security is just another racist policy designed to strengthen a fascist manifestation by the Republicans. On the subject of President Donald Trump's border wall, history professor Rudy Koshar wrote, "When Donald Trump screams, 'I am building a wall,' he is doing more than creating another sound bite or exploiting Republican-built hatreds toward minorities.[7] With an impressive degree of political instinct, he is tapping into the essential nature of classical fascism." Koshar performs an astonishing dumb politics feat by suggesting that Republicans have a pre-built hatred toward minorities while linking any notion of border security to classical fascism. Yet Koshar sums up a popular radical-perceived notion of those who want to improve border security. Take comfort in the fact that Koshar holds a platform at the University of Wisconsin-Madison, where he can pass this kind of dumb politics rhetoric onto your kids and to young naive minds for generations to come. Of course, universities are not exactly the arena for diverse political conversations, as I will examine in another chapter.

Even political representatives that directly share the border with Mexico buy into the assimilation of dumb immigration. Democratic Representative Beto O'Rourke of El Paso, Texas stated that a border wall to help protect the safety of American citizens against the potentially harmful effects of illegal immigration is a "racist reaction to a racist myth,[8] the myth being that drugs don't come in from Mexico. But a woman was busted in El Paso for attempting to enter the U.S. from Mexico with nearly $1.6 million worth of meth in 2016.[9] A 75-year-old woman was arrested when she tried to smuggle nearly 17 pounds of heroin in 2018.[10] These are just two of many examples of the drug and sex trafficking trade routes that flow heavily through El Paso. Mr. O'Rourke gets a check mark for his astuteness in dumb immigration.

Former Democratic presidential candidate Bernie Sanders described the proponents of border security as "bigoted" and "xenophobic."[11] This is a politician who represents the state of Vermont, which is 96.7 percent white, making it the second whitest state in America. Even John Tucker of the Peace and Justice Center in Burlington, Vermont stated that there is a lack of job opportunities and cultural offerings that keep minority populations away. Tucker even related moving to Vermont as a minority is like Jackie Robinson when he broke baseball's color barrier.[12] Yet Bernie wants to dictate the immigration policies of those bordering states and dares to call those proponents of stronger security "bigots" while we wait for him to propose a solution that sends more illegals to his perceived xenophobic state.

Bernie isn't the only politician using dumb politics to shame those bordering states, which range from 68-74 percent white populations, for their supposed intolerance to minorities. Democratic Representative Carol Shea-Porter from New Hampshire stated that President Trump's position on immigration, along with that of his supporters, has "disregarded" the "tolerance for religious and ethnic diversity of our nation."[13] New Hampshire is not exactly the mecca of immigrants and diversity, either, considering it is 96 percent white. But dumb politics lets you preach about the ignorance of those bordering states with the most diversity in race and culture while you're in your 96 percent plus white population state.

Scrutiny on immigration policies is not reserved just to the United States. Even Mexican officials who can't control their own corrupt country want to dictate U.S. policy on immigration. Mexico Foreign Secretary Luis Videgaray stated that any walls along the border are a "hostile" and "deeply unfriendly" act. Not only is border security racist and fascist, it is also aggressive, hostile, and just downright mean, according to Mexican officials. Even former Mexican President Vicente Fox called any border wall for security a "racist monument."

Criticism comes from as far away as North Korea, which has called our immigration policies and the U.S. in general "the worst-ever tundra of human rights in the world and the ringleader and the mastermind of human rights violations" and stated that, "to make things right, the U.S. should take responsibility and allow those refugees to enter the country, settle them down, and guarantee the minimum living condition."[15] Yes, dumb politics has North Korea, one of the most repressive governments in the world with no institution of individual liberty, in agreement with political leaders and activists that it is inhumane for our country to enforce border security.

However, it is not just individuals who have the responsibility of ensuring the border is protected. It is the duty of the federal government to protect states from foreign invasion, regardless of how "inhumane" one party or another country deems it to be. Article 4, Section 4 details these responsibilities as follows:

> "The United States shall guarantee to every State in this Union a Republican Form of Government, and shall protect each of them against Invasion; and on Application of the Legislature, or of the Executive (when the Legislature cannot be convened) against domestic Violence."

Protecting against invasion may sound like a preemptive measure against some kind of foreign military occupation of a state, but that is not what is specifically expressed in this section. As written, this means that if 400,000 Canadians decided to cross into Minnesota, it is the government's job to protect against that invasion. With the establishment of sanctuary cities, and those cities releasing illegal immigrants back into society after they have committed criminal acts, the federal government has failed to uphold Article 4, Section 4.

One of the major questions surrounding this issue is if illegal immigrants have the same rights as American citizens. Those who believe in the equal protection of illegal immigrants will cite the 14th Amendment, which is written as follows:

> "All persons born or naturalized in the United States, and subject to the jurisdiction thereof, are citizens of the United States and of the State wherein they reside. No State shall make or enforce any law which shall abridge the privileges or immunities of citizens of the United States; nor shall any State deprive any person of life, liberty, or property, without due process of law; nor deny to any person within its jurisdiction the equal protection of the laws."

The idea derived from the language of the 14th Amendment is that illegal immigrants have rights under the statement that no state shall "deprive any person of life, liberty, or property, without due process of law." More specifically, they are protected under the word "person," which applies to anyone, citizen or not. Opponents will say the word "person" is defined in the beginning of this amendment as those born or naturalized in the United States. Whichever argument you support, the fact is that only the former concept is being supported and that is that illegal immigrants have been equally protected and have shared many of the same basic rights as American citizens.

Rational or not, this certainly has not been a deterrent to illegal immigration. There is little to deter illegal immigrants from coming over and staying in our country—that and we have always been a nation of amnesty. Amnesty continues to have ongoing support for those who reside in the U.S. illegally. A study done by GenForward looked into what 1,800 Americans ages 18-34 thought of our current immigration policy. Eighty percent favored a path to citizenship for undocumented immigrants currently living here. That means a whole other generation will support amnesty, and those who are able to enter illegally know they have a chance to stay for good. So why wouldn't immigrants make the dangerous journey and take the risk, knowing that they can anchor into America and let time determine their status? This is where the issue of illegal immigration becomes a humanitarian crisis that falls on the United States to solve. Nobody likes deporting people. Nobody enjoys separating families. Nobody likes the mess required to secure a border. Yet it is necessary to preserve the freedom and opportunity that this country has to offer. Despite the repeated bumper sticker arguments, mounting empirical evidence shows that there is an ongoing crisis spilling onto our side of the border and it demands reinforced security.

THE VIOLENCE

Despite the more than two billion dollars in foreign aid the U.S. has been providing Mexico through a useless program designed to battle issues associated with drug distribution and trafficking called the Merida Initiative, violence continues to plague their nation in record numbers. In fact, 2017 was the most violent year for Mexico in two decades, with a reported 29,168 murders, a 27 percent increase from 2016.[16] Mexico continues to suffer from instability, as elected officials are plagued with ties to the cartels. These cartels now run Mexico. They have destroyed tourist destinations, corrupted law enforcement and wreaked havoc on local citizens. Their violence has no threshold. These are not just murders, but brutal atrocities that include torture, beheadings, dismemberment, and mass executions.

The barbaric nature of these cartels was once believed to be unique only to those radical terrorist groups such as the Islamic State of Iraq and Syria (ISIS). Yet, it is now happening in our own backyards and has even moved into our homes. The cartels have been responsible for close to 179,000 confirmed murders since 2006.[17] That is equivalent to wiping out the population of Jackson, Mississippi. These stats don't include countless kidnappings, missing persons, and other senseless acts of violence. Their targets can be anyone from mayors to reporters to innocent men, women, and children. More than 350 corpses were discovered in Durango in 2011 and 2012, and included a former mayor of the municipality of Tepehuanes, Durango.[18] Since 2003, the National Association of Mayors states that 47 mayors have been murdered in Mexico for daring to stand up against cartels or getting in their back pocket.

Hundreds of journalists have been killed due to their coverage or lack of coverage on cartels. Ricardo Monlui Cabrera, a journalist, was murdered while walking with his wife for being outspoken on government corruption.[19] Gumaro Perez Aguilando was another journalist shot to death at his six-year-old son's school Christmas pageant.[20] Miroslave Breach, one of three journalists killed in the month of March 2017, was shot eight times in her car outside of her home for exposing possible cartel connections with political figures in Chihuahua.[21] A total of 11 journalists in Mexico were senselessly slain in 2017. As of May 2018, a total of six reporters have been killed, making journalism a very dangerous practice in Mexico.[22]

Murders in Mexico by organized crime have an endless horizon. Cartels are only thinking of more creative ways to kill and torture their victims. The Sinaloa Cartel has literally thrown living people out of airplanes. In July 2016, the Los Zetas cartel massacred 20 victims that included four children, five women and two men. Three of those victims were Texas residents. As if that wasn't enough, the gang members even executed the family dog.[23] Cartels dumped 35 partially bound and fully nude bodies on a downtown road during rush hour in Boca Del Rio. Another group dumped 49 tortured bodies, with heads, hands, and feet removed, on a road in Cadereyta Jimenez.

If they are not dumping bodies in the middle of the street, they are digging mass graves throughout Mexico. A ranch 40 miles outside of Texas was found to contain 500 body parts that had been partially dissolved in acid. In 2014, 43 students were kidnapped off buses in Iguala for seemingly no reason other than that the authorities that stopped them had connections with organized crime in that area. It is left up to the imagination on what happened with those students. Unless you know what the cartel is capable of, that imagination can come up short. Witnesses have testified that cartel enforcers dismembered children and forced parents to watch as intimidation tactics. This was the exact case of Marciano Millan-Vasquez, a member of the Los Zetas cartel, who dismembered a six-year-old in front of her parents so they can "remember me" before ordering the murder of them.[24]

My home state of Texas has given many of us Texans a unique perspective and concern over security that is not shared by other states. Texas shares 1,254 of the 1,900 miles of the border between the U.S. and Mexico. The state with the second most miles of shared border is Arizona, which covers 372 of the 1,900 miles. To say that Texas has a concern for border security is a substantial understatement. In 2016, a 26-year-old was shot dead while fishing on a lake that borders Texas and Mexico. On that same lake in 2010, a man was shot in the head while jet skiing with his wife, who managed to escape. The investigation for this particular murder experienced a major stall when the lead investigator was decapitated and his severed head was delivered in a suitcase to a military post near the Texas border.

The excess violence in Mexico is coming even closer to our Texas cities. As recently as 2017, a family was caught in the crossfire between cartels and Mexican marines in Nuevo Laredo, leaving two little girls dead. In the same year and month, a mother was killed and her three-year-old son was shot in the leg during a shootout in Reynosa, a town near McAllen, Texas. These cities that border Texas are becoming more and more dangerous. As a DEA agent put it, "If you walk into any of the border cities right now other than Nuevo Progresso, then you are putting yourself in the cross hairs. You know you will become a target." The list of horrendous murders and crimes can go on and on, but here is the fact: 5,700 Americans were killed in the U.S. by cartel-related violence from 2006 to 2010. By comparison, 2,349 Americans were killed in Afghanistan and 4,487 Americans died in Iraq.[25]

Not all violence is cartel-related. In May 2017, three illegals were arrested after they kidnapped a Texas attorney in Orange County in the middle of the night and took him to a local bank to empty out his account.[26] A 21-year-old man was shot in the head while working the graveyard shift at a convenience store by an illegal who had faced deportation proceedings two years earlier.[27] In 2010, an 18-year-old man was tortured, strangled, beaten and doused with gasoline before being set on fire by an illegal classmate.[28]

In 2002, Ronald da Silva was shot and killed by an illegal alien who had been previously deported. Da Silva's mother, Agnes Gibboney, applied for immigration with her family three times before finally being granted legal status into the United States, only for her son to be killed by an illegal immigrant. Not only that, but her son's killer is set to be released in 2020.

Grant Ronnebeck was murdered by an illegal immigrant in 2015 over a pack of cigarettes while working at a convenience store in Mesa, Arizona. The man who shot him was out on bond from a previous conviction while the U.S. Immigration and Customs Enforcement (ICE) Agency determined whether or not he should be deported.

Perhaps the most infamous example was the murder of Kate Steinle in 2015 by an illegal immigrant who had been deported five times, which lit a spark on the validity of sanctuary cities. Again, the list of these unfortunate crimes can go on and on. Yet just one murder by an illegal immigrant being protected by cities and officials who are blatantly ignoring the law in the name of dumb politics is enough to demand accountability at our border.

Insufficient border security has also contributed to the growth of some of the most notorious gangs in the US, most notably the Mara Salvatrucha gang, better known as MS-13. Most detractors will state that MS-13 is comprised of El Salvadorians or other Central Americans such as Hondurans and Guatemalans. They will state that only a small percentage of illegal MS-13 members are Mexicans and the border with Mexico is not a contributing factor. Though it is true that most of the illegal MS-13 gang members are not Mexican, it is also true that those who are illegal are not exactly hopping on United Airlines and touching down in the U.S. with ease. Instead, they are making the journey from Central America through Mexico to America.

Even though MS-13 has become an "American" gang, its ties go deep with the cartels in Mexico. The Sinaloa drug cartel in Mexico hired MS-13 gang members to kidnap and torture two teenagers accused of stealing their drugs from a stash house in St. Paul, Minnesota.[29] Texas DPS Gang Threat Assessment has classified MS-13 as a Tier 1-level threat due to its extreme levels of violence, transnational criminal activity, and their ties to Mexican cartels. This is a gang whose motto is "mata, roba, viola, controla," or "kill, steal, rape, control." This is a gang that runs child prostitution rings. This is a gang whose signature weapon is a machete like that used on four young men ages 16-20 who were massacred in New York in 2017 and whose bodies were so mutilated that it was difficult to identify them. This is a gang that has been using the revolving door that is the U.S. border to strengthen their numbers and effectively do business with the cartels of Mexico. Government leadership seems to not mind holding the door open to strengthen the power of this infamous gang in the name of righteousness or gaining illegal votes, the latter being the preference.

America needs to regain control of its borders to defend its citizens from the senseless violence that pours into our bordering cities as well as cities all over the country. This is not intended to say that all illegal immigrants are dangerous criminals. Many keep to themselves and avoid trouble in an attempt to steer clear of deportation. Many come to this country to become a net benefit to society by working hard at the opportunities presented.

Plenty of crimes are committed by Americans. There is no reason why we need to import more crime. Those who are ignorant on immigration try to present those who look to reform the policy as xenophobes who classify all illegals as violent and dangerous criminals. Again, if one murder or death from an illegal immigrant could have been prevented, that would have spared many the misery of that act. How many more Americans must suffer to get our sovereignty taken seriously? Of course, the violence from cartels and the gangs have one central element that fuels their madness. That central element is one that Americans cannot get enough of: drugs.

THE DRUGS

Just how bad is America's drug problem? Drug deaths have been rising in all 50 states from 1999-2014. In 2014, 47,000 Americans died from drug-related deaths. In fact, drug-related deaths have killed more people than guns and car accidents for a while now. Americans love to get high and love to do it to excess.

The largest contributing factors are prescription opioids and heroin. This has become an epidemic in America. The CDC reports that, in 2015, nearly 13,000 people died from heroin-related overdoses, an increase of 20.6 percent from 2014.[30] In 2016, more than 15,000 died from heroin-related overdoses. The main source of these drugs that are killing Americans is Mexico. Mexico now dominates the heroin market in the U.S. The 2015 National Drug Threat Assessment states, "Southeast Asia was once the dominant supplier of heroin in the United States, but Southeast Asian heroin is now rarely detected in U.S. markets. Mexico and, to a lesser extent, Colombia dominate the U.S. heroin market, because of their proximity, established transportation and distribution infrastructure, and ability to satisfy U.S. heroin demand."[31] Mexico has taken over the supply and production of heroin and distributes it through a border that is easily exploited, while Washington debates its reason for existence. Even former Homeland Security Secretary Jeh Johnson said that drugs are getting in now "by land, not sea."

What's more concerning is the production of Fentanyl, a synthetic opioid pill mixed with heroin that's been linked to an alarming rate of overdoses, like that of famous musician Prince. Fentanyl is said to be 25-50 times more potent than heroin and 50-100 times more potent than morphine. It is cheaper, more potent, and easy to overdose on. The Mexican cartels and their foot soldiers in America are successfully peddling these drugs to the young, old, male, female, and all kinds of different demographics. Even Joaquin "El Chapo" Guzman, head of Mexico's largest drugs cartels, once boasted, "I supply more heroin, methamphetamine, cocaine, and marijuana than anybody else in the world."

Dumb politics proponents ought to be proud that they made these international criminals so successful and continue to undermine any attempt to eliminate the drug trafficking routes into this country. The most common route taken to transport drugs into the U.S. is by vehicle. Drugs are stashed in secret compartments such as tires, gas tanks, and door panels. The next most common route is by people carrying drugs on foot, better known as "mules." The U.S Border Patrol seized 15,182 pounds of heroin, 10,273 pounds of methamphetamine, 6,174 pounds of cocaine, and 857,888 pounds of marijuana in 2017 at the border sectors with Mexico.[32] It becomes confusing when lawmakers are so inherently against a barrier that could disrupt the flow of drugs that made it past our borders. No one is saying a wall will stop all drugs coming into the U.S. If there is a demand, there is a way. But a barrier can make drug smuggling more difficult and costly, and that cost is then passed on to consumers. If there was ever a case to build a wall, it is supported by the tides of deadly substances flowing into our country.

What is even more troubling is the fact that there are many of those who believe there should be absolutely no borders. *Salon*, a super trendy far-left website, posted a piece reaffirming the beliefs in open borders titled, "Everyone's wrong on immigration: Open borders are the only way to defeat Trump and build a better world." Perhaps it would be a better world for those 948,000 Americans who reported using heroin who would have easier and cheaper access to the drugs of their desire.[33] The article goes on to declare that "A wall is a fantasy, not a reality, that makes us economically and politically weaker. None of the moral grounds for exclusion make any sense, despite our knee-jerk resort to national sovereignty."

In dumb politics and dumb immigration, it is a knee-jerk reaction to want to decrease the $64 billion worth of drugs that comes into the U.S. every year. It gets worse as the article states:

"Migration is a human right. A person anywhere in the world has the right to migrate, just as there is a right to free speech or association. In fact, most other rights follow from the right to migrate. If governments are allowed to lock up people behind walls, then it's only a matter of time before other rights will dissipate, too. If we do not recognize migration as an inviolable human right, and if we do not give up the idea of the wall, we are bound to lose human rights for all of us."

The border wall in the U.S. is not the same as the Berlin wall. It is meant to keep people out, not keep people in. Yet the author of this article believes that a person anywhere in the world has the right to free speech, making their worldly opinion on the subject a little less reliable.

This is not a fringe ideology that is only shared by extremists. Prominent members in the political atmosphere share this extremism. Keith Ellison, the vice-chair of the Democratic Party's Progressive Caucus and U.S. representative from Detroit, Michigan, wore a tee shirt with the words "Yo No Creo En Fronteras" during a May Day parade in

Minneapolis. The slogan means "I Do Not Believe in Borders."

New York Mayor Bill de Blasio called for the abolishment of ICE. What exactly is the purpose of ICE? Direct from its website, ICE's mission is to:

> "Protect America from the cross-border crime and illegal immigration that threaten national security and public safety. This mission is executed through the enforcement of more than 400 federal statutes and focuses on smart immigration enforcement, preventing terrorism and combating the illegal movement of people and goods."

Twenty-eight-year-old Alexandria Ocasio-Cortez won a shocking victory in a Democratic primary for United States Congress as a major underdog with a platform that included the abolishment of ICE. Ocasio-Cortez is a candidate who has the support of the Democratic Socialists of America. This is a group whose New York chapter tweeted out, "Abolish profit, Abolish prisons, Abolish cash bail, Abolish borders #AbolishICE" on June 29th, 2018. It is one thing to call for the abolishment of ICE and borders, but it is a whole other level of stupidity to call for the abolishment of profit, prisons, and bails. Though only 2,780 people liked this tweet, it is 2,780 people too many. This is an easy demonstration of the level of aptitude of the individuals who support eliminating borders and ICE.

While a barrier and an increase of security at the border will never stop 100 percent of the drug smuggling, you can rest assured that the elimination of ICE and an open border policy will stop nothing. This is a country that already suffers from an average of 115 American deaths every day due to opioid overdoses.[34] Surely the free flow of drugs is not a policy that should be advocated by anyone, much less those that hold office. Nonetheless, by promoting the abolishment of border security, they are doing exactly that.

THE DRAIN

Illegal immigrants are not exactly highly taxable citizens. Actually, they are not citizens at all so therefore they are not taxable. Undocumented workers cannot receive a social security number; thus, they cannot file taxes through traditional methods. This has not been proven to be a deterrent for undocumented workers to become employed. Employers are not allowed to ask to see any specific documents from a worker other than what they provide. While employers are required to verify the eligibility of new hires, illegal immigrants can simply provide a fake Social Security number or use someone else's. The employer can report a false W-2 but the IRS rarely investigates these matters due to the high numbers of questionable W-2s and limited amount of resources to investigate all cases.

Some illegal immigrants do file taxes, such as those who have been issued a Social Security number via work visa or temporary status. While some do pay taxes in the hope that it will someday help them achieve permanent status, many are paid "under the table" for their work. Imagine if you are an illegal immigrant, and you could either pay no taxes or pay and, hopefully, possibly become a legal citizen. The former seems more likely than the latter. However, if you are an illegal immigrant and cannot get a Social Security number, the IRS still has you covered. In 1996, the IRS created the Individual Taxpayer Identification Number (ITIN) for non-citizens ineligible to obtain a Social Security number. This allows undocumented workers the ability to contribute to the economy and the opportunity to collect refundable benefits such as the Child Tax Credit. The Additional Child Tax Credit (ACTC) allows illegal immigrants to claim a $1,100 credit per child if they have a valid Social Security number. For children that do not have a Social Security number, families can qualify for a $500 credit.

Prior to the 2017 tax cut by the Trump administration, children were not required to have a Social Security number to receive the full credit.

With any public benefit comes fraud. The Treasury Inspector General reports fraud payments ranging from $5.9 billion to $7.1 billion, as well an instance where nearly 24,000 ITIN payments went to the same address.[35] IRS data from 2015 showed the agency received 4.4 million income tax returns from workers who do not have Social Security numbers. In 2015, there were an estimated 11 million illegal immigrants in the country. Not even half, much less the majority, paid taxes on income.

In 2017, the Federation for American Immigration Reform reported that it cost taxpayers approximately $134.8 billion to cover the costs incurred by the presence of illegal immigrants. This is compared to the total $18.9 billion in taxes paid in by illegal immigrants. That means the total economic impact of illegal immigration is $116 billion in the negative.[36] It may be the popular decision, but it certainly is not the rational one, to provide undocumented workers with such benefits. The goal for politicians is to be seen as compassionate and caring, despite the damage it causes American taxpayers and, more so, those who fought and earned their way into the country, only to subsidize those who broke in.

One could argue that illegal immigrants help stimulate the economy by spending money here and paying sales taxes. However, money is being sent back to their home countries in large amounts. That means that whatever tax credits and benefits we give illegal immigrants are done only to have those benefits benefiting another country. Why would we continue to do this? Because dumb politics has led us to believe it is the moral and superior thing to do. These transfers of cash from the U.S. to other countries are known as remittances. The amount reached $69 billion in 2016, according to data compiled by the Inter-American

Dialogue, a D.C.-based think tank. In 2017, $26.1 billion alone was sent to Mexico, more than the $24.1 billion sent in 2016.[37] These are the latest figures reported by Mexico's Central Bank.

The weak currency of Mexico is one of the main forces behind money leaving our country. This is just another example of one of Mexico's problems becoming our problem. Remittances are outperforming manufacturing and oil exports for top sources of foreign income in Mexico. So the only entity that benefits from this is the country of Mexico. There is no incentive for them to help control our borders if money is being sent and spent in their economy. These remittances have become a very unfavorable consequence of the illegal immigration problem we have in the United States. It does not do the country any good if $26.1 billion is being made in our country, only to be shipped back out to Mexico.

When you combine dumb immigration with the workings of dumb economics, you start to hurt the American worker. It is true that any increase in the supply of workers in a particular skill group lowers the wages of that group. Illegals are willing to work for less pay, meaning it keeps the price of labor from increasing, especially if there are mass influxes of illegals. It has been found that a 10 percent increase of workers reduces wages by at least 3 percent.[38] What is more, an increase of workers can have more of an impact on a particular group than on others. Take, for example, that a 10 percent increase reduces the number of native-born black workers by 5.1 percent. It also has the largest negative impact on wage earners who lack a high school diploma in America.[39] Native wage earners have to compete with illegal immigrants for work. In order to compete, they must be willing to work at equal or lower wages. This happens to both low- and high-skilled workers. This may lead to the belief that employers are exploiting illegal immigrants to keep wages low. But these are practical business decisions they make, similar to individual citizens choosing products or services that will give them the most bang for their buck. Saturation of our labor force devalues the American worker.

We can have sound immigration without burdening taxpayers and wage earners. We are a sovereign nation that gets to pick and choose who comes into our country. This is not a bad thing; do not let dumb immigration tell you otherwise.

MEXICO'S POLICY

The United States is its own standard. Our culture and foundation have made the U.S. an attractive destination for immigrants all over the world seeking opportunities that may not be present in their current country. However, our own citizens tend to seek the policies and structure of other nations. Whether it is health care, tax rates, redistribution, or education, citizens like to measure the U.S. against other countries. In many areas, pundits love to point out the supposed shortfalls of the United States compared to other countries, even if those countries lack many of the same demographics, culture or structure of the U.S., which is required to give a true apples-to-apples comparison. Yet these evaluations persist and are used to push a particular issue in a direction that favors their agenda. An example can be seen when so-called democratic socialists cite false positives of socialism in Nordic countries, which will be discussed further in the Dumb Economics chapter.

If this game is going to be played, it should at least be played fairly meaning, if someone is going to cite positives of one country to support a particular issue, they should be willing to hear policies that go against their single line of thinking. Using this same tactic of comparison, one can take a measuring stick to illegal immigration policies of the United States versus Mexico, specifically the laws that govern acts of illegal immigration that are specifically laid out in Mexico's constitution. Using the World Intellectual Property Organization database, we can look exactly at what Mexico has to say in its constitution about illegal immigration and see how the United States falls short by comparison. Article 32 of their constitution reads:

"The Law shall regulate the exercise of the rights granted by Mexican legislation to Mexicans who possess other nationality and shall issue provisions to avoid conflicts of double nationality. The exercise of offices or functions which, as provided in this Constitution, require the incumbent to be a Mexican by birth, is reserved for those who fill such qualification and do not acquire other nationality. This reservation is also applicable to cases established in other laws enacted by the Congress of the Union. No alien may serve neither in the Army nor in the police or public security forces in times of peace. Only Mexicans by birth may be active members of the Army in times of peace, and of the Navy or Air Force at any time, or hold any office or commission therein. The same requirement of being Mexican by birth shall be an indispensable qualification for captains, pilots, chiefs, machinists, and all crew members of any merchant vessel or aircraft under the Mexican flag or insignia. Such status shall also be a necessary qualification to hold the offices of port authority and all steering services, as well as the office of airport commander. Under equal circumstances Mexicans shall be preferred over aliens for concessions of all sorts and for all government jobs, offices or government commissions where the qualification of citizenship is not indispensable."

In the above Article, the constitution bans non-native born immigrants from holding certain jobs that gives preference to native-born citizens and even prohibits foreigners from participating in the military during peace time. The next article to examine is Article 33, which states:

"Aliens are the ones who do not have the qualifications set forth in Article 30. They are entitled to the constitutional rights granted under Chapter I, Title First of this Constitution; but the President of the Republic shall have the exclusive power to compel any alien whose permanence he may deem inconvenient, to depart from land territory immediately and without any previous hearing. In no way may aliens intervene in the country's domestic political affairs."

The above Article gives the president of Mexico the power to deport any foreigners at any point as deemed necessary without any kind of immigration hearing. In the U.S., we are lucky if anyone even shows up to these types of hearings.

Mexico used to have some of the strongest and most prohibitive laws on immigration that were set forth in the Mexican General Law of Population. These laws included things such as being able to ban foreigners from the country if their arrival upsets "the equilibrium of the national demographics" or were considered unfit to be citizens, whether from behaving poorly, becoming criminals, or "not found to be physically or mentally healthy." Foreigners were only admitted to Mexico "according to their possibilities of contributing to national progress" and they must be able to have the ability to adequately fend for themselves and their dependents. Illegal immigration into Mexico was considered a felony and came with a penalty of up to two years in prison with a fine of 300 to 5,000 pesos. Penalties from those who were deported and who attempted to re-enter the country without authorization included possibly being imprisoned for up to 10 years. There is no doubt Mexico had much stronger penalties for illegal immigration than the U.S.

Many of those policies of the Mexican General Law of Population were replaced by the Migratory Act of 2011. This act was geared to be a more "progressive" reform to a strict immigration policy. This liberally watered-down Act serves as the basis for illegal immigration today. These changes included enacting a merit-based point system for residency, efforts toward a more humanitarian admissions system, lighter penalties for illegal entry, equal access to Mexican courts, and reduced local law enforcement on immigration.

However, that has not stopped Mexico from keeping illegal immigration in check, particularly on immigrants from Central America. This is not a bad thing. Let's be honest, Mexico is just in the way of Central American immigrants getting to America so their illegal entry is hoped to be only temporary. If Mexico has stronger enforcement at its borders then so does the United States. Statistics from the Migration Policy Institute show that in 2015 and 2016, Mexico apprehended tens of thousands more Central Americans than the U.S. did at the border.

Amnesty International is a non-governmental organization whose core values are focused on forming "a global community of human rights defenders based on the principles of international solidarity, effective action for the individual victim, global coverage, the universality and indivisibility of human rights, impartiality and independence, and democracy and mutual respect." According to Amnesty International, Mexico is in violation of human rights because of their immigration policies. In an article on the Amnesty International website titled "Mexico: Migration authorities unlawfully turning back thousands of Central Americans to possible death," they state that Mexico is "routinely turning back thousands of people from Honduras, El Salvador and Guatemala to their countries without considering the risk to their life and security upon return, in many cases violating international and domestic law by doing so."[41]

Even with a lighter policy, Mexico is still seen to have harsh immigration law enforcement, enough to be considered a violation of human rights by Amnesty International. Through Mexico's previous policy, current constitution, and current tough enforcement of immigration at the southern border, it is only fair to make a comparison of the two countries. If Mexico can be tough on immigration, so can we. It is their right as a sovereign nation just as much as it is ours. That is not to say that each country should turn a blind eye to those in detrimental hardships around the world. It is to say that each country has the ability to set the standards on who they let in, how many they let in, and when.

CONCLUSION

There is nothing racist about wanting to protect citizens of your own country. There is nothing xenophobic about trying to stop the violence, drugs, and welfare abuse that come from unsecured borders. There is nothing bigoted about wanting to protect American workers. The issues of illegal immigration come from a practical standpoint, not an ethical one. But just because it is practical does not make it unethical. There is not an immigration problem in the U.S. in a way that suggests we do not accept enough immigrants. The United Nations estimates there are 46.6 million people living in the United States who were not born in the U.S. Germany is the next largest with about 12 million immigrants.[40] That means the U.S. has almost four times as many immigrants than the next largest leading nation.

The good news is that there are polls that show people do not support the extreme, which is an open border policy. A 2018 Harvard-Harris poll found that 76 percent of registered voters do not believe the United States should have open borders, and 61 percent said current U.S. border security is inadequate.[42] Yet the concern is that these ideas are shared less by millennials. A survey conducted by GenForward in 2017 found that millennials tend to believe that current border security does not need any enhancement. This can be seen when you break down the races of the millennials. Only 57 percent of white millennials support the government increasing spending on security and enforcement at the border. It is even less with other racial groups. Only 42 percent of African-Americans, 44 percent of Asian-Americans, and 37 percent of Latinx support increased spending at the border. Millennials support a wall at the border even less. Twenty-three percent African-American, 22 percent Asian-American, 15 percent Latinx, and 40 percent White millennials support building a wall to stop illegal immigration. Millennials are now the largest generation of Americans and have become the most ethnically and racially diverse generation. They represent the future of American policy. Dumb immigration policies and rhetoric will impact how this issue is handled in the future. If there is not more support for border security, dumb immigration will win and these negative consequences will only fester.

CHAPTER 4—DUMB ECONOMICS

There are no greater examples of unintended consequences than those seen in economics. This theory can be seen in journalist, economist and philosopher Henry Hazlitt's book "Economics in One Lesson." Hazlitt uses the "broken window" example to demonstrate a simple economic consequence. The example goes like this: If a hoodlum throws a brick into a shopkeeper's window, the economic gain would go to the window repair company that now has business to fix that window. This repair company is paid $250, which it then uses to pay other merchants or suppliers, and which then continues down the line of opportunity to others who have benefited from this broken window. Some might say that the hoodlum provided an economic service and benefit. What is not examined is that the shopkeeper intended to buy a new suit with that $250. Instead, the shopkeeper did not buy the suit and used the money to fix the window. The repair company's gain of business is the tailor's loss of business. The shopkeeper had the ability to purchase a suit but instead had to forgo a suit to replace a window that already existed.

No one sees the loss of business to the tailor because dumb economics will never see a suit not being made. It only sees a new window.

A simple yet impactful example shows how policies can benefit one group at the expense of other groups. There are consequences to every tax increase, new regulation, wage increase, stimulus, and economic policy. Consequences can be good or bad and can live out in the short term or long term. As citizens, we tend to measure only that which we can see and immediately account for in economics. Gains want to be measured immediately in economics.

This is no different than for unemployment. Everyone wants to see unemployment decrease. There have been proposals and politicians who support the idea that government should guarantee jobs to all citizens. People see unemployment, rather than seeing the government offer a solution to eliminate unemployment. Guaranteed jobs and zero unemployment at first sight would seem like a remarkable thing. It is a heroic thing, enough to make government a new "Avenger" in the Marvel movies and comics. The government would be able to guarantee a job for Thor, even though he is an illegal alien.

What is not seen is a tax hike to support and pay for these jobs. That is taking money out of the private sector that could have been spent on investments as well as other goods and services. What is not seen are the consequences of a sudden wage inflation from the government guaranteeing jobs at a guaranteed minimum pay. Private industry will suddenly have to compete for labor against the government, which will pay more for low wage earners, meaning companies will have to increase their wages, which will, in turn, increase costs to consumers.

What is not seen is how this is contrary to how the market for labor works today. Instead of having work and needing labor to help produce, the government hires without having any work and nothing to produce. Guarantee jobs now and find work later. There are only so many infrastructure jobs the government can produce. This leads to temporary work and, when that work is done, taxpayers will be paying for workers to do artificial work with no benefits. No private company would hire someone without having real work to do. In private practice, every hire is a net benefit to the company's output. What is not seen is that low unemployment might be more productive than guaranteed government jobs because, though there is still unemployment, those that become employed produce more economic output than the government could ever produce at zero unemployment. The result is good, short-term benefits with long-term consequences.

I use the government-guaranteed job as an example because it has been a recurring idea in politics and has the support of 46 percent of Americans in 2018.[1] It is one of the many examples of issues that Americans tend to see as a moral benefit to the economy. It is just another example of looking at the short-term impact of a single group. Dumb economics will look at other examples of how short-term and short-minded narratives influence bad economic policies. Henry Hazlitt summed up his lesson in one statement: "The art of economics consists in looking not merely at the immediate but at the longer effects of any act or policy; it consists in tracing the consequences of that policy not merely for one group but for all groups."[2]

MINIMUM WAGE

Votes come easy and cheap when politicians' acts of compassion and caring are geared directly toward synthetically raising the earnings of minimum wage employees. These acts are deceitful and repulsive in nature because politicians take advantage of the blissfully ignorant group at the expense of others. These tactics are merely performed to secure votes because, if you ignore the unintended consequences, raising the minimum wage sounds like a damned good plan, especially if you happen to be a voter making that minimum wage. Dumb politics uses terms like "living wage" to establish a rivalry between employee and employer.

This line of thinking usually assumes this is the case of the small impoverished employee versus the gluttonous large corporations such as McDonalds, Walmart, Target, Amazon, Pizza Hut, etc. But there is no rivalry. Both parties have to make money and, if one party does not (employer), then neither does the other (employee). Large corporations have a lot of resources and capital at their disposal, but they are not invincible. Raising the minimum wage would still be a substantial cost to them, but they have the ability to counterbalance some of those costs through different resources. For example, many corporations have high-powered tax attorneys to help find loopholes within the system to avoid high taxes and help offset the costs. They also have special interest groups and lobbyists in Washington to advocate for them and gain political favors. Corporations have the capital to invest in automated processes and systems that eliminate costs. Simply put, they can invest in a machine that squirts ketchup on a hamburger rather than pay the overhead of an employee to do so. Increasing the minimum wage would certainly expedite those investments into automated processes.

That being said, these corporations would rather not deal with the process and costs associated with raising the minimum wage. One adverse effect would be the need to raise wages across all employees. Now that the minimum wage employee makes close to the amount the manager makes, the manager would expect a raise in wages, then the manager's boss would expect an increase, etc. With no increase in output or value from employees to justify wage increases, these businesses suffer and pass their expenses on to the consumer, cut hours of employees, or simply put up the out-of-business sign. That is what dumb economics does—it entitles the employee to more money without any increase in productivity at the expense of the employer and consumer.

Not all companies are built to sustain government interventions that fix the cost of labor. Rising costs of labor and its effects do not apply just to large corporations with an abundant amount of resources to help adjust. Small businesses see the most significant impact. Barbershops and family-owned hardware stores do not have any of the large corporate capital or political pull to offset costs. A $15 minimum wage would be devastating to their businesses. The little café would have to raise its prices to offset costs, which would drive away customers. Profit margins are extremely thin in the service industry as is, and even more so with small businesses, no matter the vertical. The family-owned restaurant cannot afford as many employees, and will have to cut hours and personnel. The local bicycle shop will turn away those with little to no work experience, even if they are willing to work at a lower wage. What good is a minimum wage increase if you cannot work or work full time? If I told you I make $300 an hour, you would think, "Wow, you're awesome," but then I say I only work one hour per week and suddenly it's, "Wow, that sucks."

There is no benefit to minimum wage with the combination of higher prices, less hours per week, and an increase in unemployment. Small businesses account for 55 percent of all jobs and 66 percent of all new net jobs since the 1970s, and provide jobs to 8 million people, according to the U.S. Small Business Administration.[3] A report from the Harvard Business School titled, "Survival of the Fittest: The Impact of the Minimum Wage on Firm Exit," found that each $1 increase in the minimum wage results in a 4-10 percent increase in the likelihood of a restaurant closing.[4] It is no wonder that the prospect of raising the current federal rate of $7.25 to $15 strikes fear in the hearts of

many business owners. That fear is realized in many states and cities that have increased their minimum wage laws locally. There are
so many examples on how the minimum wage increase impacts small
businesses that it could fill an entire book.

Consider Tastes of Life, a nonprofit and faith-based restaurant,
which closed its doors after a minimum wage increase in Michigan.
Terri Tucker, who managed the restaurant's finances, stated that "...for
us to have stayed open we would have really had to have raised prices
by about 40 percent and we would have needed another two or three
hundred customers a month to come in."

ARGYLE Haus of Apparel had to move its business to Las Vegas
due to the increased minimum wage in California. Founder Houman
Salem sums it up by saying, "California's putting up the going-out-of-
business sign. It's a tragedy."[5]

Almost Perfect Bookstore used a profit-sharing model to its
employees that actually benefited the employees more than the mandatory increase in minimum wage to $15 an hour. Once the minimum
wage increased, the company saw fewer profits, meaning employees
received less of the profit share, which led to an actual decrease in
their paychecks despite an increase in hourly earnings. After 25 years,
Almost Perfect Bookstore closed its doors for good in 2016. Only in
dumb economics can workers earn less while making more hourly.

Who does this hurt more than anybody? It hurts teenagers and
young adults who encompass a significant amount of the entry-level
workforce. Low-skilled labor is highly elastic, meaning a change in
wage has a large effect on demand. This is a simple debate on the law
of demand which no politician, economist, or consumer has been able
to argue or disprove. Artificially high wages for low-skilled workers
show less demand for employment. Essentially, they are priced out of
a job and lose valuable learning experience to help set up a successful

career path down the road. Many of those teens or young adults are in college and depend on a good number of hours per week to help get by. Sure, they will make more money per hour but they will work less per week. This means they could be making less, even with the higher pay per hour. That's if they even receive work in the first place.

A University of Washington study found that Seattle's increase to $13 an hour, part of a phase to get minimum wage to $15 an hour, led to a reduction of hours for workers, which lead to lower pay. This study found that, "The lost income associated with the hour reductions exceeds the gain associated with the net wage increase of 3.1 percent.... [W]e compute that the average low-wage employee was paid $1,897 per month. The reduction in hours would cost the average employee $179 per month, while the wage increase would recoup only $54 of this loss, leaving a net loss of $125 per month (6.6 percent), which is sizable for a low-wage worker."[6]

So, if a student is making more per hour but less per month, then the minimum wage has failed at the very thing it was trying to achieve; more money back into the workers' pockets. Then what happens when college students see their hours cut in half? They can't afford college, so they take out a larger loan, setting them up with more debt. Or they will drop out of college completely and miss an opportunity at a higher education, which means less skilled and educated workers in the workforce. This negative outcome is not limited to just college kids. For some, it is a living. George Reisman, PhD, Professor Emeritus of Economics at Pepperdine University, summarizes the effect of a minimum wage of low-skilled workers during a time when the Obama administration was considering a minimum wage increase from $7.25 to $10.10:

"At today's minimum wage of $7.25 per hour, workers earning that wage are secure against the competition of workers able to earn $8, $9, or $10 per hour. If the minimum wage is increased, as you and the President wish, to $10.10 per hour, and the jobs that presently pay $7.25 had to pay $10.10, then workers who previously would not have considered those jobs because of their ability to earn $8, $9, or $10 per hour will now consider them; many of them will have to consider them, because they will be unemployed. The effect is to expose the workers whose skills do not exceed a level corresponding to $7.25 per hour to the competition of better educated, more skilled workers presently able to earn wage rates ranging from just above $7.25 to just below $10.10 per hour. The further effect could be that there will simply no longer be room in the economic system for the employment of minimally educated, low-skilled people."[7]

An increase in minimum wage hurts low-skilled workers and adversely hurts the poor. Employees suddenly have to compete with government intervention while business compete to stay open.

Raising the minimum wage has unintended consequences and it is easy for young people to look past that line of thinking. They see more money and not much else. Economic prosperity is not achieved through government intervention. Growth is achieved through productivity and, without an increase in productivity, employers do not have the means to justify a wage increase. In fact, if those who wish to see wealth distribution can take McDonalds CEO, who makes $21.8 million, eliminate his salary and spread it across their 375,000 employees, you have successfully given those employees an extra $58 in their pocket for the year. Even if 150,000 of the 375,000 were minimum wage earners, they get a whopping additional $12 each month in their pocket for the year. Those wanting to live a more prosperous life should not depend on the government to get them there. In addition, one should not demand more from those more successful to supplement their wages without any justification other than "they make too much money." That is not just dumb economics; it is envious, pathetic, lazy, and an irrational attempt at an entitlement that does not exist.

The simple truth is that some people will earn more than others for many different reasons. What is often seen is that people making minimum wage, compared to those in the top 20 percent of earners, is only a difference of age or stages of life. Most people do not make the same income their entire life and, if they maintain a work history, their experience certainly does not remain constant. The chances of income turnover at every stage give workers the ability to go from rags to riches, as well as the chance to go from riches to rags. Employees can find an abundance of resources to make themselves more valuable to employers. The idea that the consent of a wage between an employer and employee is dictated by a third party leads to an entitlement instead of a value. New goods and services are created every day to compete for consumption. Same for employment; as goods make our lives better, productivity makes us more valuable to employers. Only competition can make you prosperous. It is why some choose to go to Ivy League schools or receive post-graduate degrees, so they increase their value and earn more throughout a lifetime.

Without any additional output of productivity to justify an increase in minimum earnings, employers adjust in ways that do not favor the employee. The best intentions don't always lead to favorable results. A $15 minimum wage is not the product of the millennial generation or generation Z (better known as the iGen). Raising the minimum wage has the support of prominent members in D.C., such as Nancy Pelosi, Bernie Sanders, Chuck Schumer, Hillary Clinton, and Elizabeth Warren. This has become another generationally backed issue that stirs the pot of entitlement in the form of artificial wage increases. Politicians can guarantee a particular wage all they want, but they cannot guarantee a job or hours for workers—only the amount of money workers can make if they get that job.

TAXES AND REDISTRIBUTION

If I were to tell you that Person A pays $20 in federal income tax and Person B pays $40 in income tax, but Person B earns twice as much as Person A, would you think that's fair? A reasonable person would agree that it seems fair that Person B pays twice as much, considering that Person B makes twice the amount of money. An equal tax rate is justified since both earners enjoy the same benefits of taxation such as infrastructure, parks, police protection, and other amenities needed for everyday life at the expense of the federal government. Yet this is not an example of the progressive tax system that exists today; instead, it is a proportional tax rate, better known as a flat tax. Obviously a 50 percent tax rate is high but, for the sake of demonstration, it illustrates a true example of paying your fair share.

Our system is designed so that the more you earn, the less you keep. There will always be a plethora of people who believe that we need to keep less, distribute more, and move toward a centrally planned system. Some even cite false examples to push this narrative. Presidential candidate Bernie Sanders, a self-proclaimed Democratic Socialist, believes the United States should emulate Scandinavian countries that match his perceived idea of socialism. In an interview with George Stephanopoulos, Bernie stated, "Well, so long as we know what democratic socialism is, and if we know that in countries, in Scandinavia, like Denmark, Norway, Sweden, they are very democratic countries, obviously. The voter turn-out is a lot higher than it is in the United States. In those countries, health care is the right of all people. And, in those countries, college education, graduate school is free." This is one of the many attempts Bernie used to generate buzz around his socialist beliefs. There are a few problems with this. Number one, Scandinavia is not socialist. These countries are capitalist markets that do not nationalize production. They are simply capitalist countries with heavy taxation. They practice what is called the Nordic Model, which is defined by Investopedia as follows:

> The social welfare and economic systems adopted by Nordic countries. The Nordic model combines features of capitalism, such as a market economy and economic efficiency, with social benefits, such as state pensions and fair income distribution. This model is most commonly associated with the countries of Sweden, Norway, Finland, Denmark, and Iceland.

Even Danish Prime Minister Lars Løkke Rasmussen said, "I know that some people in the U.S. associate the Nordic model with some sort of socialism," he stated. "Therefore, I would like to make one thing clear. Denmark is far from a socialist planned economy. Denmark is a market economy."

Nima Sanandaji is a writer on *The Stream* who grew up in Sweden and had this to say in a piece titled "5 Myths about Nordic Socialism Peddled By the Left."

> "When it comes to areas such as business regulations, trade policy, investment freedom, vouchers in the provision of education, elderly care and health care, and partial privatization of retirement savings, Nordic countries are among the most free-market in the world. In fact, in these areas, the U.S. has a lot to learn from Denmark and the other Nordic countries."[8]

The second issue is that the population of Sweden, Norway, Finland, Denmark, and Iceland are the following respectively: 9.82 million, 5.35 million, 5.54 million, 5.75 million, and 337,000. These countries make up about one-twelfth of the U.S. population. Not to mention that there are still 45 percent of Americans who do not pay income tax and 11 million illegal immigrants. Scandinavia does not have the same representation of diversity and social structure as the U.S. It has one of the most homogenous populations. There is no basis that a Nordic Model, again not to be confused with socialism, would work in the U.S.

This model has not produced the economic utopia that supporters hoped to see. These countries have their share of problems just like the U.S. Sweden had one of the highest growth rate in the late 1800s to mid-1900s after embracing a free enterprise capitalist system. After the 1970s, Sweden began to roll back its business-friendly enterprises and started to impose higher taxes, more regulations, and redistributive social policies. Sweden went from one of the top five richest countries to not even the top 10.[9] This is why some of Sweden's largest companies, such as Volvo, were started nearly a century ago and this country has not seen much innovation since. High taxes are why the CEO of famous furniture store IKEA left Sweden for Switzerland and moved the IKEA headquarters to the Netherlands.

After the Nordic countries, it is hard for Bernie Sanders or individuals who support his economic policies to point to examples where socialism works. Those in dumb economics will happily ignore the self-destruction seen in the socialist state of Venezuela in favor of promoting an idea theoretically and morally corrupted.

All of the problems that Venezuela is experiencing are the exact problems that come from long-term socialism. This is a country that has trouble keeping the lights on and sees rapid scarcity of basic goods such as bread. Inflation skyrocketed by 800 percent in 2016 and reached 25,000 percent in 2018. Consumers have to hoard food while the price of these goods continues to rise. In fact, food is in such short supply that an estimated 75 percent of Venezuelans lost close to 20 pounds in 2016. This forced weight loss program was dubbed the "Maduro Diet," in reference to Nicolas Maduro, who became president after Hugo Chavez's death. The shortage of food has caused Venezuelans to literally dig food from the trash so they can eat. You take one look at Nicolas Maduro and you can see that he and his political allies are certainly not digging for scraps.

How could a country, in one of the greatest times in our history, bring itself to this much poverty and misery? As soon as Hugo Chavez came into power, the government took control of industry after industry. The thought is that government can better provide and dictate what the people need more than the people themselves; this is a key staple of a socialist regime. Chavez promised to run these businesses better than private industry and would share the profits with the citizens. A combination of high tax rates and government takeovers caused businesses, money, and people to flee the oppressive reach of the Venezuelan government. Then the government ran out of people's money to take as socialist governments always do. Venezuela's entitlement programs grew so large that they collapsed underneath their own weight.

There are many examples of failed socialism from the past and from the present, yet many continue to ignore the consequences. Twentieth-century socialism came with a great deal of poverty, along with tyranny. But there are always politicians, college grads, professors, progressives and others that believe their version of socialism will come with more love, caring and sharing. Socialism is just a broken-down car with a different driver that believes he or she can run it more efficiently. It is amazing how many people still cling to the socialism utopian fantasy. This fantasy is not far from realization if those who are willing would take up residence in North Korea, Cuba, or Venezuela. You have one country that is ruled by a merciless dictator, one that is stuck in a time capsule, and another that cannot even feed its own people. Each of those countries is alike in those same regards.

We hear a lot about how the top one percent owns ninety percent of the wealth in America, or some sort of rhetoric along those lines. What you do not hear is that those earning $250,000 or more pay nearly 52 percent of all federal income tax. What dumb economics fails to recognize is that the additional tax revenue collected from property taxes (you never truly own property because you are a tenant on government land and will be forcefully removed if you fail to pay that tax), sales tax, capital gains tax, death tax, estate tax, state income tax, etc. all get higher as you earn more, assuming you buy more expensive belongings and purchase larger real estate. Considering all these variables, U.S. citizens pay in excess of 50-60 percent of their money in taxes, including income tax.

In Venezuela, those who created wealth either created it in other countries or simply left Venezuela altogether. When there is no one left to tax at the rate of spending, the system collapses under itself. It is not a matter of if it will happen; it is a matter of when.

Higher earners are not the only ones susceptible to high taxes under socialism. Bernie Sanders' tax plan would have had single individuals making $50,000 a year paying $5,000 more in taxes. Millennials fresh out of their dumb economics college class would state that those individuals would receive more in benefits, such as free health care and college. But what if individuals are healthy and/or do not want to go to college? They still have to subsidize others who receive those benefits. They do not have the choice to opt out.

The idea of lowering taxes typically gives way to headlines such as: "Tax cuts will lead to a $1 trillion-dollar deficit." The main driver behind these headlines is the Congressional Budget Office (CBO), whose forecasts often miss their mark. The CBO tends to assume behavioral habits will remain stagnant despite the fact that tax reform has shown changes in behavior for both consumers and businesses. This is why the CBO has continued to vastly underestimate growth such as it did during the Reagan tax rate reductions and the cutting of capital gains tax from 28 percent to 20 percent in the 1990s.

Behavioral economics studies the decision-making processes of individuals and the driving factors behind each of those decisions. Certainly, one would assume that economic behavior changes when there is more money in an individual's pocket from paying less taxes. This is seen in investments where investors opt for tax-exempt securities; a lower tax rate could change their behavior and lead to them investing in investments that have an opportunity to produce a higher rate of return while being susceptible to taxation. It is difficult to predict these behaviors, especially when the CBO and other entities only measure a tax cut based on dollar figures that fail to measure economic behavior.

Take some of the examples out of Thomas Sowell's book, "*Basic Economics—A Common Sense Guide to the Economy.*" Sowell points out that, when Maryland passed a higher tax rate on those earning a million dollars a year or more, the number of people living in Maryland fell from nearly 8,000 to fewer than 6,000. Despite an increase in the tax rate and the projection that there would be a rise in tax revenue of $106 million, what actually happened was revenues fell by $257 million. This increase changed the behavior of those earners who opted to move out of a high taxation state, leading to a smaller pool of millionaires that could be taxed. Oregon experienced a similar problem in 2009 when it raised its income tax rates on people earning $250,000 or more. Oregon's income tax revenues fell by $50 billion. In addition, when Iceland gradually reduced its corporate tax rate from 45 percent to 18 percent, its revenues tripled between 1991 and 2001.[10]

The debate over taxation has given dumb economics the ability to establish class warfare that excludes any reform idea not associated with an increase in a progressive tax system. It has become more important to look at taxes, as some polls have shown upward of 58 percent of millennials favor either socialism, communism, or fascism over capitalism. Economics has shifted from a practical study to a moral theory. Capitalism is thought of as selfish and greedy, with producers marked as the central enemy. The discouraging reality is that it has become a growing consensus to feed off of those who produce, and that parasitic mentality begins with taxes.

THE LAFFER CURVE

In the discussion of taxation, there is one question that can never be answered, and that is, what is the optimal tax rate? Dumb economics says that a high tax rate can always be higher and those who make the most ought to pay the most. But perhaps the question should be, what is the optimal tax rate to generate the most tax revenue for our government?

There is a popular concept in economics known as the Laffer Curve, which was developed in the 1970s by Arthur Laffer, a prominent economist who served on Ronald Reagan's Economic Advisory Board. The Laffer Curve shows the relationship between tax revenue and tax rate. The concept is so simple a child can understand it. The curve is displayed in figure 1A. The horizontal line represents

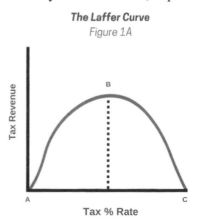

The Laffer Curve
Figure 1A

the tax rate the government imposes. The vertical line is the tax revenue received from that tax rate. At point A, which represents a zero tax rate, the government makes exactly zero revenue. No taxes, no revenue. Simple enough. However, point C shows what happens when the tax rate is 100 percent. If your income was taxed 100 percent every day you went into work, what would you do? Well, you would not work unless you loved giving all your money to the government, which is not a popular consensus. If there is no one working at the 100 percent tax rate, there will be zero tax revenue.

The key is to find the optimal tax rate that will yield the government the most tax revenue shown at point B. Anything after or before the optimal rate means the government collects less revenue. The Laffer Curve has a downward U-shaped curve, making it very difficult for those deep into dumb economics to understand the fact that, after point B, the government collects less revenue despite higher tax rates. Is it so crazy to suggest that higher tax rates can lead to less tax revenue? Dumb economics proudly says yes because it ignores the consequences of an absurdly high rate.

After point B, people start funneling money through different avenues to avoid taxes, such as setting up offshore accounts or using an inflated tax code to work against it. Or it can stunt growth and the upward mobility of earners and spending. Even this graph begs the question: what is the optimal tax rate to generate the most tax revenue for our government? At what rate is that critical point B on the graph? Many economists believed that this point on the graph was 70 percent. Anything over a 70 percent tax is when the government starts to lose money.

Consider a more relevant study done by Christina D. Romer and her husband David H. Romer. Christina Romer, served as chair of the Council of Economic Advisers to President Barack Obama. Both she and her husband are highly regarded economists serving in the Economics Department at the University of California, Berkeley. Their study, titled "The Macroeconomic Effects of Tax Changes: Estimates Based on a New Measure of Fiscal Shocks," was published in *The American Economic Review*, which is one of the most prestigious journals in the world. This study showed that point B is located at 33 percent. It showed that each 1 percent above 33 percent resulted in a reduction of up to 3 percent in gross domestic product (GDP). This study combats the notion that the optimal tax rate can always be more.

The Laffer Curve applies to corporations as much as it does to individuals. In 2017, Sen. Chuck Schumer (D-NY), an astute member of dumb economics, stated "no one in America, not the American public and not the economist, believes that trickle-down works," as if to speak for everyone. This was in response to the GOP's 2017 tax cut plan and specifically the corporate tax cut. He then went on to state that tax breaks "don't lead to job creation; they lead to big CEO salaries and money for the very, very wealthy." Sen. Schumer targeted AT&T for not passing tax savings to their employees and failing to create more jobs. Almost immediately, AT&T announced that it would give a bonus of $1,000 to more than 200,000 employees and invest an additional $1 billion into the United States once President Donald Trump's tax plan was passed. Many companies followed suit on passing these corporate tax cuts directly on to their employees. Companies such as American Airlines, Apple, Bank of America, Comcast, Discover Financial Services, Home Depot, Starbucks, Verizon, Walmart, Walt Disney, Waste Management, and numerous others trickled their tax savings to their thousands of employees in the form of cash bonuses, increased retirement contributions, or shares in company stock.

When you ask most people what the optimal rate is, one side will simply state that the rich need to pay their fair share while the other cites the 16th Amendment (the ability for Congress to have the power to collect taxes on incomes) as unconstitutional. Whatever side you are on, there still remains the fact that point B exists and the current rate of 37 percent for top earners today may be too high. If you are under the belief that the rich should pay more of their fair share, the question becomes, what is their fair share? Is it 20, 30, 40, 50, 60 or 70 percent? The answer typically is not met with a numerical answer but instead it is responded to with the simplicity of "more." Dumb economics cannot wrap its head around the idea that lower rates lead to economic growth while producing a trickle-down effect that leads to higher revenues. When President Ronald Reagan cut taxes, total revenues increased by 99.4 percent during the 1980s and income tax increased by 54 percent by 1989. Even John F. Kennedy, one of the left's most admired presidents, stated "it is a paradoxical truth that tax rates are too high today and revenues are too low, and the soundest way to raise the revenue in the long run is to cut the tax rates." Like Reagan, Kennedy's tax cut plan across top and bottom earners stimulated higher tax revenues.

Who are the top earners in the U.S.? What comprises those greedy rich people in the top percent of earners that dumb economics demands pay their fair share? If you want to be in the top ten percent, you need to make a household income of around $160,000. While this amount is comfortable, a couple living together, with each making around $80,000 a year, probably would not consider themselves rich by any means. A household income of closer to $200,000 can be considered top five percent. While a great living, it still does not qualify as the fat cat, cigar-smoking, money-hungry savages portrayed by politicians. Yet research shows that those who earn $100,000 and above pay nearly 80 percent of all income taxes in the United States. Those who make above $100,000 typically have some serious debt, whether it be from schooling or opening a business with a loan. In dumb economics, it makes sense to tax the hell out of them for continuing to self-improve.

Tax rate increases on the rich are only symbolic forms of increasing revenues which, in reality, are more geared to securing votes than actually raising revenues. The issue of taxes is not a zero-sum game in which one group can gain something at the loss of another. There can be a win-win scenario when revenues increase as tax rates and government spending decrease. No matter if it's a tax cut or tax increase, both policies must be met with spending cuts. Spending, not tax cuts, creates deficits. If you lost your job and settled into a lower paying job, you would not or should not continue spending at the rate of income from your previous employment.

DEFICITS

What creates a deficit in your personal income? Spending money on a car you cannot afford or not receiving a raise at work? Both happening simultaneously would certainly cause a deficit, but spending money you do not have always causes a deficit, even if you are a multimillionaire or make trillions, like our federal government. The CBO reported a $665 billion deficit despite receiving $3.3 trillion in revenues in 2017.[11]

While the Laffer Curve is a great example of increasing tax revenue, what is the point of increasing revenue when it justifies more spending? Tax cuts should force the government to be more fiscally responsible. It is hard for those inundated by dumb economics to imagine that the government may not use increased revenue on social welfare programs or infrastructure. Those who want to raise the tax on top earners are only encouraging, and even enabling, more government spending. You do not need an economics degree to know that the more you earn, the more you typically spend, and sometimes overspend. It is why lottery winners are more likely to declare bankruptcy within three to five years than the average American.

It should not shock taxpayers that the government would intentionally or unintentionally waste funds. Every year, Sen. Rand Paul puts out a glorious report titled "Airing of Grievances," which details a lot of the wasteful government spending. The 2017 report included examples such as the National Science Foundation spending $1.5 million to improve how tomatoes taste, and the U.S. Agency for International Development spending $14,833,312 on developing foreign versions of Sesame Street to teach kids around the world about things such as "climate change awareness." Speaking of climate awareness, the U.S. Agency for International Development spent $11,441,758 to promote green building and development in Vietnam. Sen. James Lankford developed a report in 2017 titled, "Federal Fumbles," which listed over $473 billion in wasteful spending. These reports only scratch the surface of wasted government resources. There are more than 400 agencies, departments and sub-agencies in the government. Each of these entities employs who knows how many actual useful employees and contractors. In fact, our own government does not even know the extent of government agencies. The Administrative Conference of the United States naively stated:

> "[T]here is no authoritative list of government agencies. For example, FOIA.gov [maintained by the Department of Justice] lists 78 independent executive agencies and 174 components of the executive departments as units that comply with the Freedom of Information Act requirements imposed on every federal agency. This appears to be on the conservative end of the range of possible agency definitions. The United States Government Manual lists 96 independent executive units and 220 components of the executive departments. An even more

inclusive listing comes from USA.gov, which lists 137 independent executive agencies and 268 units in the Cabinet."[12]

Under Barack Obama's presidency, the national debt grew by about $9 billion. While some of that debt is attributed to George W. Bush, there is no doubt that, during the Obama administration, debt skyrocketed to nearly double the amount of debt when he took office. However, much like those before him and most likely those after, Obama continued a long-standing tradition of adding to the national debt. These costs are passed on to citizens either directly in the form of taxes or indirectly in the form of high rates of inflation. True fiscal conservatives are lacking in Congress or, if they do get elected to office, they certainly are insignificant in influence. Government is guaranteed to get its money one way or another up until your death, so spending is always guaranteed.

SOCIAL SECURITY

If there was ever a true entitlement program that we as citizens deserve outright, it is Social Security. Ever since you and I landed our first jobs, we have been paying into this program. Dumb politics believes Americans are not capable of making smart financial decisions on our own. Instead, dumb politics believes the government can better save for your retirement than you can. It is the government that can manage your money better than you can. It is the government that has your retirement plan's best interests at heart. At least, that is what those in dumb politics who practice dumb economics believe. Does anyone still truly believe this?

Social Security has become the largest expenditure of our federal budget. Comparatively, the government spent $590 billion on national defense and $939 billion on Social Security in 2017.[13] This program of one generation has become the financial burden on many generations to come. Ironically, when President Roosevelt signed the Social Security Act in 1935, he declared that this "will act as a protection to future administrations against the necessity of going deeply into debt to furnish relief to the needy." Instead, government is going into debt furnishing the relief of everyone that has paid into this program, not just the needy. There is a reason 81 percent of millennials believe that they will not collect Social Security benefits.[14]

Much like any other economic policy pushed by an administration, the long-term consequences were not thoroughly considered. Robert Myers helped frame the Social Security program in 1934 and detailed the thorough analysis used to establish 65 as the age at which one receives full benefits. He wrote that, "Age 65 was picked because 60 was too young and 70 was too old. So we split the difference."[15] That is how deep was the thinking that went into a program that has become the largest expenditure of our government. When this program was signed, the average life expectancy was around 60 years old. If a person happened to live above average life expectancy, they certainly would not be collecting Social Security very long. The average life expectancy did not hit 65 till around the early 1950s.

Today, the life expectancy average is nearly 80, which means many more people are collecting Social Security for many more years. There used to be 159 workers for every 1 retiree receiving benefits. According to the Social Security Administration's own website, there are now 2.8 workers for every 1 retiree.[16] Yet this program will not go broke or run out of cash. When have you known of a government program this large to cease to exist or operate in the net positive? In 2018, self-proclaimed leftwing media watchdog group, Media Matters, claimed that Fox News had been using fearmongering to spread the idea that Social Security will not exist for future generations that pay in. Media Matters stated that, "Beginning in 2034, as the trustees' report notes (not 2022 as the FOX segments claim), Social Security faces a problem of not having enough revenue to pay out full benefits—but it can be addressed without cutting benefits by simply raising additional revenue."[17]

That is the simplest solution to any government issue: just simply raise additional revenue. Raising additional revenue is a nice way of saying raise taxes to keep funding it until it is broke again, then raise taxes some more. But Media Matters is right; that is the answer the government will likely take, which is why there is the belief that Social Security will always be around. This was a program that used to pay back more in benefits than recipients paid in Social Security taxes. This is a program that pays an average monthly check of $1,404. That is a whopping $16,848 a year to live off of during retirement. For perspective, this is just above the poverty line for a two-person household, which was at $16,240 in 2017. The fact is that not many people can sustain their lifestyle near the poverty line at retirement.

The contributions into our Social Security system are not contributions at all. They are taxes used to fund other government expenditures, not just Social Security. Our payroll taxes are not invested into our future like those true contributions of other retirement funds such as a pension or 401(k). These taxes do not go into a single account dedicated to each individual, even though research has shown that 32 percent of Americans think this.[18] For years, the government has been accused of dipping into the Social Security Trust Fund for non-related funding. Even former Speaker of the House Paul Ryan had this to say about government interfering with the future of younger generations' Social Security: "…stop the government from raiding surplus Social Security tax dollars to pay for other programs and give younger workers the chance to get as good a deal from Social Security as current retirees get."[19]

For a government program designed to fund elderly Americans to retire, you will not find a financial adviser in the world that would suggest you to plan to live off of Social Security. Unfortunately, there are no options to opt out of this program. We are forced to pay into this, despite shelling out more in taxes then we will collect in benefits. This is even more true with millennials and the generations that will follow. However, it does not benefit society when millions of Americans are struggling to get by and working well into their retirement years. Retirement savings and investment strategies need to be taught and instilled early on in our education system. Becoming dependent on a government program is not going to work for much longer. It has not been working, considering my generation will not receive anything near the benefits for the Social Security taxes we paid. That's because the ratio of those paying into Social Security taxes now is becoming less and less. Only self-determination and discipline can insure you have a prosperous life even during retirement.

CAPITALISM

There are many myths surrounding the idea of capitalism and free trade. The idea that capitalism favors the rich over the poor, exploits workers, drives poverty, paves the way to tyranny, is inherently immoral, is routed in selfishness, etc.—these are all myths perpetrated by ignorance. The main difference between capitalism and other principles is driven by one element: incentives.

Capitalism is quite the opposite of selfish. It is a trade-off and a voluntary transaction between you, another individual, or a business. You provide something for me and I provide something for you. Company A has the incentive to develop a great product that will generate demand because, if it does not, then you will not purchase that product.

Suddenly, Company B creates a better product incentivizing Company A to improve its product or be driven out of the market. Incentives breed competition and competition makes our lives better. Is it such a horrible thing for companies to strive for higher profits? This is a great age for capitalism; consumers are more informed about products and services they purchase than ever before. It is hard for companies to ignore the massive amount of reviews and research widely available for all consumers. This changes everyone's economic behavior. Capitalism has helped companies become more transparent in their products, it has helped advance more innovation, and has geared products to more consumer satisfaction. Capitalism forces businesses and entrepreneurs to meet the needs of customers. That sounds pretty unselfish to me. In return, we give them profits.

We can measure profit on how well those businesses achieved meeting the needs of others. Look at the example of Uber. This is a company that was founded in 2009 and has already hit the mark of $37 billion in gross revenue in 2017. Uber took an outdated industry and turned it on its head. I have yet to hear from someone that prefers using a taxi over Uber. It is not just Uber, either. As consumers, we enjoy our iPhones, being able to easily shop on Amazon, research on Google, stream entertainment from Netflix, or post on Facebook, Snapchat or Instagram. These are all great innovative companies brought to you by capitalism. Some of them are relatively new, with only 10 to 20 years of existence. All of them are centered on making consumers' lives easier, more efficient, and enjoyable.

Can you imagine going to Blockbuster to rent and return your movies or shows? Can you imagine still using one of those Nokia brick cell phones? Government cannot run businesses more efficiently because they lack the same incentive as private industries. There is no need for innovation when consumers are forced to use your services and have no other options. Look at the case of FedEx. If the government had complete control over shipping and package delivery at the USPS, we would be stuck without many of the great innovations that FedEx pioneered. The founder of FedEx, Fred Smith, had the simple yet bold idea to have packages shipped overnight. This was not even considered a reality at the time by anyone, much less the United States Postal Service (USPS). Smith put these ideas into action and now we are able to enjoy the luxury of having packages shipped to us in a hurry. Not only that, but FedEx gave consumers the ability to track packages real-time. USPS's greatest innovation over the years was their move to start delivering on Sundays, which started in 2014.

When government nationalizes an industry, there is simply no incentive to innovate or innovate quickly to stay ahead of competition because there is no competition. America is not a free market economy, yet its mixed economic policies have led to the innovation and growth of some of the largest companies in the world. Forbes put out a list of the World's Largest Public Companies in 2018. Twelve American companies made it into the top 25, more than any other nation. Not only that, but these companies employ millions of people, which provide the opportunity of prosperity that no government program can match. We need to continue working toward a system that drives competition and innovation because it is better for workers, consumers, and citizens.

An example can be taken from the Baltic countries, specifically Estonia. After the fall of the Soviet Union, these countries achieved capitalist freedom. Estonia has become one of the most business-friendly countries in Western Europe. When Estonia lost its independence under the Soviet Union occupation, GDP was only about $2,000 per capita in 1987. The Soviet Union left Estonia's economy in shambles per the norm with socialist policies. This led Estonians to opt for radical change that would distance itself as far away as possible from a Soviet Union-type market.

After its independence and elections held in 1992, Estonia did exactly that. The results were astonishing, considering this was a country that many believed would dissipate without the dependency on Russia, which accounted for 92 percent of Estonian international trade. A combination of free market policies, flat tax rates, and an entrepreneur-friendly environment led to major growth for this country. In 1992, Estonia had about 2,000 enterprises; by 1994, this figure rose to 70,000. Estonia has seen an average of six percent economic growth every year since its reform. Poverty is down, standard of living is up, and overall quality of life is on the rise. Estonia's GDP has since surpassed Russia, which still remains a corrupt and centrally planned hole. As of now, the GDP for Estonia is $31,500 per capita, compared to Russia's $27,900 per capita.[20] We have already seen the benefits of innovation in Estonia. Over 300 million people use Skype, which is the best-known export of Estonia. Estonia is on the forefront of technology innovation and the world is better off from them not only surviving but thriving after gaining freedom from oppressive restraint.

Capitalism has helped more out of poverty than any kind of government program out there. Socialism asks how we can help those who are living in poverty. Capitalism addresses how we get those living in poverty out of poverty. In 1965, President Lyndon Johnson declared a war on poverty in America to help those who were in the 19 percent poverty rate. Since then, the government has spent $22 trillion on programs aimed at poverty. What was supposed to be a program designed to help those people become more self-sufficient turned into a program of high dependency. The welfare state of the government has grown and discouraged those in poverty from pulling themselves out of it.

Poverty has been around 12-14 percent since 2016. The war on poverty has been lost. There has been no justification of $22 trillion of tax payer dollars to drop the poverty rate by minimal percentage points over the last 50-plus years. If you look at the living conditions of those in poverty, you can see how well off they are compared to most of the world. Using a standard set of data by the Organisation for Economic Co-operation and Development (OECD), *The Economist* measured the quality of life for the top 10 percent as well as the bottom 10 percent for a select group of seventeen countries. The United States' top 10 percent scored the best in the "Better-life index" of all countries, which should come as no surprise. However, it is the bottom 10 percent of the U.S. that is more noteworthy. Compared to all countries, the bottom 10 percent of the U.S. ranked third in quality of life, only minimally behind Canada and Sweden. What is more telling is that the bottom 10 percent ranked better than many countries that have strong social policies.[21] These countries include Britain, Germany, France, and Australia. Dumb politics often inundates us with how our current environment and capitalism in general ignores the needs of the poor. It tells us that there is too much inequality among the classes. It might be true that the rich in our nation have an exceptionally better life than others in the world. But the fact is, so do the poor comparatively. In fact, many of those considered poor in the U.S. have the basic luxuries that could not even be imagined in other countries. Consider a report done by the Heritage Foundation, which found the following:

> "The actual living conditions of households labeled as poor by Census are surprising to most people. According to the government's own surveys, 80 percent of poor households have air conditioning; nearly two-thirds have cable or satellite television; half have a personal computer; 40 percent have a wide-screen HDTV; three-quarters own a car or truck; nearly a third has two or more vehicles. Ninety-six percent of poor parents state that their children were never hungry at any time during

the year because they could not afford food. Some 82 percent of poor adults reported that they were never hungry at any time in the prior year."[22]

Bridging the gap between rich and poor does not come from class warfare and government social policies. Many blame crony capitalism, the idea that big business is buying political favors, on growing inequalities, and power of the rich. I prefer political commentator Ben Shapiro's definition of crony capitalism, which is that it simply does not exist. It is only a term used to disparage capitalism in general because there is no crony capitalism without capitalism. Shapiro refers to crony capitalism as being corporatism, which is "based on the notion that industries comprise the economy, like body parts comprise the body; they must work in concert with one another, and they must take central direction."[23]

A structure in which government connects with business to disparage competition, bring in heavy regulation, subsidize industries, and control interest is far from a capitalist ideology. Crony capitalism is a term used in defense of government expansion, as if government is free from any sort of corruption. We have seen government corruption throughout the years and, in particular, sectors in which progressives advocate nationalization—specifically in the health care industry.

HEALTH CARE

America has a nationalized health care system called the U.S. Department of Veteran Affairs (VA). This has been a program rifled with controversy, corruption, and scandal. The VA employs more than 306,000 full-time employees, runs 1,061 outpatient sites and 1,240 health care facilities, which includes 170 medical centers.[24] The VA is a monstrosity of a program with a 2017 budget of $180 billion that provides coverage for more than 9 million veterans. For a government program this large and important, it is inefficiently run, poorly managed, and has been deadly for some veterans.

In 2014, it was discovered that the VA system in Phoenix covered up a 115-day waiting period for veterans to get into their first appointment with a primary care physician. It was reported that as many as 40 veterans died waiting for care. What is more is that the officials in the Phoenix VA reported false waiting times among a sample of 226 veterans to cover their tracks. This Phoenix VA is no exception. Systemic problems have plagued the VA since its inception. These issues trace back all the way to Vietnam vet and author of "Born on the Fourth of July" Ron Kovic, who interrupted Richard Nixon's presidential acceptance speech by telling the audience: "I'm a Vietnam veteran. I gave America my all, and the leaders of this government threw me and others away to rot in their VA hospitals."

Kovic is not far off from his assessment. In 2011 and 2012, the VA hospital in Pittsburgh knew it had an outbreak of Legionnaires' disease for more than a year but decided not to warn its patients. Many patients were infected and at least five died from the outbreak. Thirty-seven patients tested positive for two forms of hepatitis and six tested positive for HIV due to poorly disinfected equipment used for colonoscopies at clinics in Tennessee, Georgia, and Florida. A dentist in a VA clinic in Dayton, Ohio admitted to never washing his hands or changing gloves between patients for 18 years. This led to nine veterans testing positive for hepatitis. Decades of corruption, negligence, and fraud have given the VA the current negative perception it has today.

The VA cannot even manage 9 million veterans. Can we imagine what a nationalized health care system for 320 million people would look like? Dumb politics can because it believes that health care is a "right" for everyone. But it is not a right. It is a necessity, just like food. We need food to survive but limited government intervention has made food affordable, accessible, and abundant, even for those in poverty. Clothing is a necessity but no one is advocating that the government should pay for it. These items are commodities and health care should be treated as such. Medical care should be demanded from medical professionals and the industry as a whole, not from the taxpayer. There needs to be more transparency in costs for medical services. With transparency, those seeking medical attention can shop from an abundant supply of providers. When consumers can shop around, hospitals will compete for their business. When hospitals compete, wait times decline, care improves, costs go down, and innovation begins. I think we can all agree that health care costs are too expensive, but the answer is not more inflated bureaucratic intervention. The answer is letting markets do the work for you, not the government.

CONCLUSION

Human prosperity is achieved and flourishes through capitalism. America has a system that rewards risk-taking, hard work, and entrepreneurship. There is no risk-taking in government and, if there is, it is done with other people's money. This is a system that has negative connotations, especially among younger Americans. There are constant studies from multiple outlets showing that capitalism is becoming less favored among millennials. A Harvard University study found that 51 percent of those between the ages of 18 and 29 do not support capitalism. Most of these unfavorable views of capitalism stem from a lack of knowledge and from older generations promising prosperity through central planning. This is a rehashed government promise that has never been fulfilled in the past and will remain dormant in the future.

Do not let dumb economics intimidate you. Arguing against minimum wage labels you as inconsiderate. Advocating lower taxes labels you as greedy. Supporting Social Security reform labels you as someone who is against the elderly. Promoting capitalism makes you evil. These are tired arguments used in dumb politics to support dumb economics. The fact is that moral grandstanding gets in the way of rational analysis. Supporting facts that help pave a way to prosperity are not always popular positions. They are not immediate, free and easy. It goes against the social norm and a culture that has been instilled into all generations.

The purpose of government is not to make you prosperous. It is not to create products and services in which the free market can do better. Governments should not be in the business of planning for your retirement. Government is not your salvation for anything. Prosperity and wealth are moving targets. Many have achieved wealth and many have lost it. People move in and out of the top 10 percent all the time. Many work hard to achieve wealth but do not work hard enough to keep it. All actions or inactions have consequences, good or bad. Economics is not a moral objective argument for bleeding hearts. We would all love more money. We would all like to retire soundly. Trying to force a utopian outcome of wealth and perfection will leave the U.S. with neither.

CHAPTER 5—DUMB EDUCATION

Our education system has been overrun by those who work in theory and live absently out of actual practice. It has become an institution of indoctrination rather than education. It is an assembly line of assimilation where kids come in, are manufactured into the product that fits their professors' ideologies, and are then shoveled out into society. There is no balance of opposing ideas and diversity of discussion. In fact, in many classrooms, people are discouraged or even shut down completely when an argument goes against a professor's ideology, as we will see throughout this chapter.

This is a growing problem in our country and it continues to get worse as this ideology inserts itself into the curriculum. At every level, we see students targeted for their viewpoints, from pre-school, elementary, middle school, high school, and most of our universities. We are training little social justice warriors to go to battle. This should be a concern among teachers and administrators, but it has not reached a level of importance. Diversity is the ultimate achievement of many educational institutions. It is a quota that can never be satisfied. Yet there is no diversity of thought. This is not a left or right issue. It just happens to benefit the left and the problem would still hold true if it benefited the right.

Many students are not challenged by anyone to think differently about many of the things teachers shove down their throats. It is all assimilation and no individualism and, when that assimilation is challenged, the consequences are not so much dire as they are sad. This leads to safe spaces, therapy dogs, trigger warnings, and other coddling techniques imposed by our education system because it has set up so many thought firewalls. Even top Ivy League school Cornell held a "cry-in" for students who could not handle the 2016 presidential election results after Donald Trump won. Students were allowed to sit and color on the sidewalks with chalk to cope with their imaginary trauma. University of Michigan Law School held a "Post-Election Self-Care with Food and Play," which gave students the opportunity to color, blow bubbles, and use Play-Doh to help these "adults" get over the election. The University of Pennsylvania brought in a puppy and kitten so students could use them for "therapeutic cuddling" for their post-election stress disorder. This is what happens when students are coddled from opinions, ideas, and thoughts that may challenge their own. We are just one more upsetting election away from a 1-800-ImTriggered hotline.

THE YOUNG

Many of us attended a school with religious affiliations such as a Catholic or Christian school. What many of us have not experienced in those schools is not being allowed to practice our religion at a religion-based school. Yet that was the case for a Christian preschool in Umeå, Sweden. The local municipality ruled that children were not allowed to say "Amen," say grace at lunch, or discuss the Bible. While it is agreed that children should not be subjected to a single type of religious theology at school, especially if it conflicts with their beliefs, the political correctness police may have overstepped their reach when they shut down religion at a Christian preschool. People have the ability to put their kids through a school that has certain religious principles that can be practiced or simply a school that practices no religion. The simple fact is that there is a choice. In dumb education, that choice is taken away.

Sweden seems to like to practice dumb education. When they are not restricting one practice, they are forcing another. There is a pre-school trend that was highlighted in the *New York Times* in which Swedish teachers actively ignore the roles of gender in their classroom.[1] This plan is part of a "compensatory gender strategy" that teaches children that gender is a supposed social construct. Instead of allowing girls and boys to participate in activities of their choosing, they are forced to do activities that are traditionally associated with the opposite gender. The goal is to stop children from identifying things as "for girls" or "for boys" and create equality in the classroom for all. This led to activities such as boys being made to massage each other's feet. Nothing says equality like forcing groups to do things they would not normally do based on their gender. But, in dumb education it makes sense.

A San Francisco elementary school implemented gender-neutral bathrooms to eliminate the differences between the sexes for kindergarteners and first graders. While the idea of inclusivity is the reason behind a lot of these initiatives, the consequences should be considered. With any decision, no matter how moral or objective it may seem, there should always be a consideration of unintended consequences. Those of us who are familiar with kindergarteners and first graders realize they often lack the capacity for rational decision making and cognitive approaches to real-life situations. Confusion that did not exist before can set in to the five-year-old boy who is forced to massage another boy's feet and use the same bathroom as little girls.

These strategies make is seem like it is meant to cause confusion. These are children who will mostly likely identify as a princess or dinosaur before they can make an identification that will be made for life. Is it impossible to teach kids to respect girls without making them act like girls? Is it impossible to teach inclusiveness without forcing them to share bathrooms? The millennial generation is one of the most inclusive and accepting generations ever. In fact, 74 percent of millennials support gay marriage, compared to 56 percent of baby boomers (ages 53 to 71) and 41 percent of those in the silent generation (ages 72 to 89).[2] As part of the millennial generation, I do not remember any kind of conditioning on "gender bias elimination" when I was a child. We did not need it. The generation after us will not need it. We all walk, talk, think, dress, and act differently. We are individuals that do not belong to a collective group based on the color of our skin, our religion, our sexual orientation, or where we were born. Nor do we all have to think alike if we have similar skin color, sexual orientation, or similar religions. I did not need a classroom and curriculum to realize that. We do not need to be force-fed our differences. We certainly do not need the government or extension of the government such as the education system to forcefully indoctrinate us in the differences of human beings, especially at such an early stage in our lives. That should not be the focus of early onset education.

These practices have been less education and more social engineering. Social engineering needs a start, and it begins at a very young age in the education system. Earlier in this book, I stated that I believe teaching our kids early and often about financial strategies and retirement is a must, considering the state of our Social Security system.

While that may never come to fruition, there are certain subjects being taught early in high school and often in college.

Edina High School in Edina, Minnesota thought it was absolutely necessary to adopt a mandatory class that helped students recognize and eliminate "white privilege." Screw teaching about management of finances, kids need to know how privileged they are. Of course, this class was described more pleasantly. English teacher Jackie Roehl, one of the course's framers, thought the class was absolutely necessary since "understanding Critical race theory was a significant reason behind our school taking another step on our equity journey—incorporating a study of Critical race theory into our sophomore English classes."[3] Her version sounds much more harmless but still fails to meet the validation of being a mandatory class. One student had a different description for the course. A popular teacher feedback website, "RateMyProfessor," allows students to share critiques of a class. One student wrote that the class should be renamed "Why White Males Are Bad, and How Oppressive They Are." Shouldn't this be enough for teachers and administrators to reconsider a course that makes one student feel as if he is a "bad" person based on the color of his skin? Is that now the norm of educational institutions where a subset of a minority group can change the policy for everyone? One student or parent feels offended by a mascot, so the whole school has to change its brand.

This happened in 2013 when a new high school was set to be opened in Draper, Utah. A number of votes were received to have the school be known as the "Cougars."[4] However, administrators and some parents thought this would be too offensive. Why? Because a cougar is also known as a middle-aged woman that likes to have sex with younger men, so that might offend them. If this sounds stupid, it's because it is. It is dumb education in its rawest form.

High school students in California were given a choice by the principal to turn their shirts inside out or go home because the shirts had an American flag on them. It was Cinco de Mayo, and administrators thought this offensive act would cause violence. The students chose to go home.[5] The affected students promptly filed suit, but a federal judge ruled that this did not violate the students' freedom of speech.

A teacher in Norman, Oklahoma was recorded telling a class of students that to "be white is to be racist, period."[6] This rightly offended a student who felt like she was being attacked based on her skin color, and led her to release the recording of the lecture to the public. The teacher went on to ask: "Am I racist? And I say yeah. I don't want to be. It's not like I choose to be racist, but do I do things because of the way I was raised." This was a lecture for a class that was intended to heal racial tensions and divides.

In Washington State, a high school football coach was suspended for taking a knee and praying silently at midfield after football games. At times, some players would even join him. After continuing to practice his religion even after his suspension, the coach was not rehired and the 9th Circuit Court of Appeals ruled that his praying was not constitutionally protected because he was acting as a public employee instead of private citizen. So, if you are a teacher, you cannot pray before eating at lunch or read a morning devotional if someone can see it publicly. This only happens in dumb education.

There are countless examples of these dumb education tactics within high schools across the world. Offense seems to only take one side and completely ignores the other. There is no equality in it. There is no room for it in education. There is no room for disparaging students based on their race, religion, or patriotism. These were liberties established long ago, yet they are being taken away again in the name of inclusion. High schools are no longer a welcome center for diversity. All the proof you would need is to either look back at your high school days or step into one of the many public institutions surrounding your neighborhood. If that is not enough, then consider where the National Education Association (NEA) tends to sway during election time.

The NEA is the largest employee association in the country, with more than three million members. In other words, the NEA has a stranglehold on public education and its influence is far-reaching. In the 2016 election, the NEA endorsed Hillary Clinton for president after taking a vote with the 175 board members. Of those board members, 75 percent supported endorsing Clinton. Before Clinton, they also supported Barack Obama back in 2011. This is an organization that does not shy away from its political affiliations. And, with more than three million members in this organization, there is going to be heavy influence in our classrooms.

Then there is the American Federation of Teachers (AFT), which has 1.7 million members. The AFT leaders supported and endorsed the Hillary Clinton campaign by a three-to-one margin.[7] And there is the United Federation of Teachers (UFT) that has 200,000 members. President Michael Mulgrew addressed a crowd of public school educators at an assembly in 2016 and announced how the UFT was going all out to make sure that Hillary Clinton won the presidency. Mulgrew stated that "we have social media volunteers, phone-banking volunteers, and door knocking volunteers."[8] We can draw the conclusion of where the UTF's political affiliations lie.

These teacher unions are powerful, large, and have a lot of support from Democratic leadership. They are embedded in the Washington, DC system with huge political contributions, special interest groups, lobbying power, and activism. Unfortunately, these unions do not use all this power to create a better educational system. Like any union, the primary objective is meant to benefit the employee, not the students. It is about the teachers' salaries, the teachers' pensions, the teachers' vacation days, and the teachers' benefits. And, of course, there is the coveted teachers' tenure. That's what unions are all about: the teachers.

There have been strikes, walkouts, and protests all around the country from teachers demanding pay raises. Teachers in Arizona went on a six-day strike that left millions of kids unable to attend school. After all was said and done, the Arizona governor approved a 20 percent raise for educators. Will students be 20 percent better in the classroom? Will education improve by 20 percent? I certainly have my doubts because none of that was part of the negotiation. However, a 20 percent raise is an amazing feat for those who work 190 days out of the year. This is not to discredit the work teachers do. They certainly deserve good compensation, but it is hard to justify substantial raises to teachers of the all-important subjects such as cosmetology, sports marketing, or sociology.

While compensation is very important, there is one fundamental aspect missing: the students. These benefits are awarded through collective bargaining agreements with the school boards, not on the performance of students the teachers teach. There is only accountability for what can be provided to the teacher instead of what the teachers can provide for the students. A website, tobecomeateacher.org, lists the benefits of teacher unions. The first benefit they list is that unions protect the rights and jobs of teachers. This is the number one benefit for the following reason: "In the past, it was not uncommon for the First Amendment rights of teachers to be grossly denied. Because of unionization—educators are now able to voice their opinions and champion causes without fear of retaliation."[9] We thought the goal of educators was to educate, not to "voice opinions" and "champion specific causes" in the classroom.

It is hard to disagree that teachers have a vital role in society and that teaching should be a well-respected profession. With any important position, whether in government or the private sector, it is still susceptible to criticism of performance and rightfully so. After all, students are only the future of this country. It is the avenue to which one generation passes on knowledge to the next and, if ignorance is rooted in the elder generation, it is implanted in the younger generation. Dumb education makes those who oppose teacher unions out to be opposed to better education.

That is far from what the issue is. There are systemic flaws within the structure of teacher unions. Problem number one: teacher union dues are collected from a portion of a teacher's salary. Up until recently, it was mandatory in 22 states that, if you were a teacher, you had to pay union dues whether you wanted to or not. This was true for all public sector unions. However, the Supreme Court case of Janus vs. AFSCME ruled that public-sector unions cannot force nonunion members to pay union dues. If a teacher does not want to be in a union, objects to the union's positions, and does not agree to the collective bargaining agreements, then that teacher should not have to pay into the union. Rightfully so, unless dumb education has you believing otherwise. Critics of this ruling argue that union funding will be largely impacted because unions' collective bargaining agreements depend on dues from union and nonunion members. The answer is, who cares? If a teacher does not agree with the union's stance on collective bargaining agreements and other activities, that is the teacher's decision.

This leads to the second problem. Teachers pay union dues by having the dues taken from their pay checks by the government. Then the government sends that money directly back to the unions. These unions are very powerful and depend on collecting dues and growing membership to become more influential. They then use this money to back candidates that support union causes. It is no coincidence that these political candidates tend to be Democrats. In fact, political contributions in the 2016 election hit the $33.2 million mark from teachers' unions. Of that $33.2 million, 93 percent went to Democrats.[10] So let's retrace. Teachers' dues are collected by the government, then paid to the unions. The unions use this money to promote campaigns that call for increasing teacher benefits and better education. If there is a particular political candidate who supports the goals of the unions, that candidate receives union contributions. Given the size of the unions, the campaign contributions are substantial, and this helps them outspend their opponents and win elections. The unions now have an ally in government to spend more money on public education that will lead to more dues that leads to more campaign contributions.

This brings us to the third and final problem: this cycle leads back to teachers' salaries, which are funded by the government, which is funded by the taxpayer. That means we are funding teachers to fund unions to fund Democratic campaigns and candidates. Dumb education likes its funding. One might argue that these unions help bring more money into the education system, which provides the funding necessary to improve schools and resources necessary to further educate. However, the government is spending $11,762 per student in public education. Some states rank even higher, such as New York, which spends more than $20,000 per student. The spend is certainly there, but what is missing are the results. In 2015, the Program for International Student Assessment (PISA) found that U.S. students ranked 40th in the world for math literacy. In science, the U.S. ranked 25th and 24th in reading literacy. The PISA measured the performance of 15-year-old students in science, math and reading in the 73 industrialized countries of the OECD.[11] The United States fell behind countries such as Vietnam, Estonia, Switzerland, Slovenia, and Macau. The government's and unions' solution of throwing more money at the education system does not seem to be sticking.

What we have are real consequences that seem to be ignored but should be concerning, no matter what your political beliefs are. We are using resources to teach young generations in our K-12 schools that, if you are white, you are racist and privileged. We are telling teachers that they cannot pray in front of people. We kick people out of schools for wearing shirts with American flags. We are focusing on the all-important issue of bathroom integration. Meanwhile, actual education levels suffer but, boy, are these new generations going to be "woke." It is a blissful ignorance being passed down one pupil at a time. It is a never-ending cycle because it begins with the teacher teaching future teachers of America.

The average age of a teacher is around 42 and that average age seems to be declining through the years.[12] Average age drops even lower at the kindergarten and elementary levels. Our teachers are becoming younger and have ideologies that are fresh from whichever higher education institution they came from. This can explain why the education system at the primary and secondary levels seems to be so single-minded. Teachers then get involved with unions, which seems to narrow their vision in education even more. These consequences have led to reforms, such as the ability for parents to decide where their child can attend school, better known as school choice.

Unions do not like school choice. It is competition and account-ability that they now have to battle. If a student is stuck in a terrible school, it should be up to the parents to move the student to a school where he or she is more likely to succeed. Why are unions so against this? Because it hurts their number one priority: the union members. They do not want to compete with other schools. They do not want parents having a choice. They want to be paid, they want their benefits, and they want to influence elections. Dumb education may sound like an oxymoron, but it is what is denigrating our public school system.

THE UNIVERSITY

Unfortunately, primary and secondary schooling is only the beginning. Dumb education starts early but certainly metastasizes in higher education. By now, most people are fully aware of the single-minded influences that take place in our university systems. However, most do not know what the extent of that influence is. The *Econ Journal Watch* published a study that looked at voter registration of 7,243 professors at 40 leading universities.[13] Turns out our assumptions were correct, because Democratic professors outnumber Republicans 3,623 to 314. This is an outrageous ratio of 11.5 to 1. When it is broken down by department, the numbers become even more revealing. It turns out dumb education has a stronghold on the university history departments and wields the ability to revise the past as they see fit. Liberal professors outnumber conservatives 33.5 to 1 in this department. The least influenced group is those in economics with the smallest gap of 4.5 liberal professors for each conservative professor. Journalism showed a 20:1 ratio and a 17.4:1 ratio in Psychology.

None of this should come as a surprise, however. I went to Texas A&M University, which is considered by many to be a "conservative" school. While the students may have shared a particular leaning, the professors and administrators certainly did not, at least in my experience. Pepperdine University is said to be a conservative school as well, yet the ratio of liberal professors to conservatives is 1.2:1. Even at schools considered to be conservative, conservatives are still outnumbered by liberals. This would not be an issue if these ratios had no effect in the classroom. But they do. Biases are taught, preached, and instilled in college students. The university is supposed to be a free-thinking forum, yet it is anything but that.

Diversity is a main objective for higher education. It is believed that people from different cultures, backgrounds, and races foster healthier collaboration, critical thinking, understanding, and promotes the ability to work well with others who are not like you. None of this is achieved if everyone thinks alike. Instead, all you have is a bunch of kids who look different but who find comfort in sharing the same world, as well as the political and social views as everyone else, including the administration. But at least they look different, so that is a win for the universities.

A great example is what happened when true diversity of thought was introduced to college campuses in 2017. Below are occurrences of some of the most dangerous and disruptive protests that happened when an outside thinker came to college campuses:

1. **The tantrum at UC-Berkeley triggered by Milo Yiannopoulos. February 1, 2017.** Say what you want about political commentator and provocateur Milo Yiannopoulos, one thing for certain is his ability to get people riled up for no reason other than just being in their presence. Yiannopoulos was scheduled to speak at the University of California-Berkeley until an irrational mob of protesters attacked the building he was in with flares, bats, and smoke bombs. One female supporter wearing a Donald Trump "Make America Great Again" hat was attacked with pepper spray directly to the face on camera. There were injuries to other students and property damage, simply because someone with a different opinion dared to show up on their campus.

2. **Dr. Charles Murray at Middlebury College was prevented from speaking through acts of violence. March 2, 2017.** Dr. Murray is a political author and columnist who was invited by Middlebury College students to speak on their campus. Predictably, this did not sit well with a large

group of students. The speaking event included a debate with Professor Allison Stanger, so each position had a chance to present arguments for various topics. Dr. Murray did not even get to the podium before an angry mob of protestors shouted him down in a series of chants and hysterical yelling. The event was moved to a secure location where the discussion could be streamed online because they were unable to continue at the current location. Of course, the free speech dissenters caught wind of the location and tracked them down. While trying to leave campus, Stanger and Dr. Murray were caught in a frenzied mob. Stanger was grabbed by the hair by one student and pushed in a different direction by another student, resulting in a neck injury that left her in a brace. Stanger stated that she had "feared for my life." Again, the mob was there to protest Murray, not Stanger. Once they made it to the car, protesters surrounded the vehicle and beat on windows, climbed onto the hood, and started violently rocking the car.

3. **NYU Protestors Pepper Spray Gavin McInnes. February 2, 2017.** Conservative comedian Gavin McInnes was scheduled to speak at New York University when his arrival was violently interrupted. A fascist anti-fascist NYU group jumped at the opportunity to prevent the free speech event. Before entering the building, McInnes was pepper-sprayed directly in the face while being swarmed by protestors. This caused an outbreak of violence that led to five arrests. McInnes only got about 20 minutes into his speaking before protesters and triggered students shut it down.

4. **Nine arrested at UC-Berkley at Ben Shapiro Speaking Event. September 14, 2017.** University of California-Berkeley was at it again. This time it was conservative

commentator and author Ben Shapiro who was endangering their feelings. Protesters formed outside the entrance to the event where screenings were being done of ticket holders. Students used tape on surrounding buildings to write, "fuck you Carol" on windows, which was directed at UC-Berkeley Chancellor Carol Christ, who has allowed speakers with different views to speak on campus. Nine protestors were arrested. Charges included carrying illegal weapons, public intoxication, battery of a police officer, battery, resisting arrest, and disturbing the peace.

While there have been many protests in 2017 and beyond, this subset garnered most of the media's attention. Conservative speakers, not to be confused with Nazis or fascist presenters, are not welcome on college campuses, which means that conservative voices are not allowed on university campuses. It is not just speaking events, either. Young America's Foundation found that liberal commencement speakers outnumbered conservative commencement speakers 12 to 1. In the top 45 schools in the country, not one of them invited a conservative to deliver a commencement address in 2018.[14] It is only fitting that college students are sent off with a commencement speech that supports one ideology from an institution that favors that same ideology. After four years (more if you were still "exploring" possibilities) of indoctrination, these institutions are not about to undo everything by having a conservative commencement address.

Universities are not producing well-rounded, critical-thinking individuals. Instead, they are producing a bunch of lemmings that get hysterical when their group think is disturbed. This has caused other students to feel like they are unable to express their individual views. A survey done by the Gallup/Knight Foundation found that 61 percent of U.S. college students agree that the climate on their campus prevents some people from saying things they believe because others might find them offensive. This is no surprise, considering that just about anything could be offensive to the campus army. This study also showed that fewer students in 2017 (70 percent) support having an open campus environment that allows all types of speech from 2016 (78 percent). To go even further, 69 percent of students believe that political conservatives can freely and openly express their views on campus. This means that both liberals and conservatives believe that conservatives are less able to freely express their views. And 92 percent of students believed political liberals were safely able to freely and openly express their views.

SAFE SPACES

There was a time when segregation on campus was aggressively fought against. Students had the right to integrate with their fellow peers, no matter their differences. Now, those intolerable so-called tolerant see it as a necessity to segregate, not just on skin color, but on thought, too. Today, it is in the form of safe spaces where blacks go over there, LGBT students go in here, liberals take that spot over there, and minorities come over here. It defeats the purpose of university inclusion, diversity, and student collaboration. It essentially tells students that it's possible to be happy all the time as long as you hide from bad thoughts.

But that is not real life. It is not how it works after college. Sometimes I think the bathroom is a safe space for me at work, then the next thing you know, someone is demanding I come out because something needs my immediate attention. Yet safe spaces are still considered a necessity among students and professors. Eighty-seven percent favor safe spaces, according to a Gallup survey. Even 70 percent of Republican students support safe spaces. The idea of safe spaces is widely embraced, even spaces that are reserved for certain races. *The Huffington Post* published an article titled, "Ethnic Minorities Deserve Safe Spaces Without White People" in response to an incident that involved two journalism students at Ryerson University being turned away from a public event because they were white.[15] The event was held by a group called the Racialized Students' Collective, which meant to have a safe area to openly discuss racialization. *The Huffington Post* article goes on to say:

> "Instead of focusing on why those students were asked to leave, we should be thinking about the history of oppression that makes these kinds of groups and these kinds of places so very important. We should be focusing on how to be aware and respectful of the rights of both the press and marginalized groups. We have to find a way to coexist peacefully."[16]

This puts the idiocy in dumb education. How can we find a peaceful way to coexist if we exclude certain races from the conversation? We can focus on the history of oppression by first trying not to repeat it. In 2016, a group of students from Pitzer College left a series of Facebook posts that insisted their roommates could not be white. It started when one female student said that anyone looking for a roommate should contact her, except for any white people. She stated the invitation was for "POC [people of color] only" describing, "I don't want to live with any white folks." Of course, this lead to a student calling her out on her racist rhetoric. One student responded back by saying "People of color are allowed to create safe POC only spaces," she wrote. "It is not reverse racism or discriminatory, it is self-preservation [sic]. Reverse racism isn't a thing."

That is true; reverse racism is not a thing. Racism is racism. Whether it is discrimination against white, black or brown, there is no reverse effect. If a white person said, "I don't want to live with any 'brown folks',," or they don't want to live with any black students so they can "self-preserve" their race (although I'm pretty sure this has been said sometime in history), it would certainly be considered racist. You can exchange the words white, brown or black with each other; it does not change its overall racist premise. Students at the University of Michigan demanded a no-whites-allowed safe space on campus designed for "black students and students of color to organize and do social justice work."[17] This demand was started by the "Students4Justice" group who "organize to target inequities on our campus." What they fail to realize is that justice starts by having a conversation with those affected and those who supposedly cause the injustice as a way to mitigate the issues.

Not all universities support this segregation. The University of Chicago came under fire when it sent out a letter in 2016 to oncoming freshmen, stating that they will not support "trigger warnings and safe spaces." A portion of the letter read as follows:

> "Our commitment to academic freedom means that we do not support so-called 'trigger warnings,' we do not cancel invited speakers because their topics might prove controversial, and we do not condone the creation of intellectual 'safe spaces' where individuals can retreat from ideas and perspectives at odds with their own.
>
> Fostering the free exchange of ideas reinforces a related University priority—building a campus that welcomes people of all backgrounds. Diversity of opinion and background is a fundamental strength of our community. The members of our community must have the freedom to espouse and explore a wide range of ideas."[18]

Bully for the University of Chicago. The letter was met with mixed reactions from students, alumni and many others. It was a refreshing take on the culture that universities have been fostering for a while—a culture that says it is okay to shield students from other students with different ideas, a culture that says it is okay to segregate students based on race, a culture that does not sponsor the same support for guest speakers of certain opinions as it does with other speakers. Instead, the University of Chicago offers a free forum of discussion and does not exclude anyone based on his or her individual traits. And yet this has become a fringe idea for a university to have. The polar opposite can be seen when the University of San Francisco launched a campus-wide social marketing campaign for students, faculty and staff to raise "awareness around social inequalities and privilege." This "Check Your Privilege" campaign asks a series of questions, such as if you are white, male, Christian, able-bodied, and heterosexual. The mission is "To increase the awareness of privilege, begin discussions around privilege, and for individuals to use their privilege(s) to advocate for others."[19] This campaign excludes all individual circumstances and backgrounds and uses a subset of broad questions to determine if a person is "privileged" before ever entering a conversation.

One of the "Check Your Privilege" campaign posters reads: "If you can expect time off from work to celebrate your religious holidays, you have Christian privilege." Dumb education believes that a religious holiday is only reserved to Christians. If you are pregnant and expect time off for maternity leave, does that mean you have motherly privilege? I doubt supporters would agree with that. This "Check Your Privilege" pomposity has spread to many universities throughout the U.S.

Safe spaces have adverse effects on racial and intellectual dialogue. They divide groups and harbor ill-conceived notions about other groups based on nothing but the generalizations that echo within these spaces. These safe spaces are becoming hate spaces that create animosity that might not have existed previously. If you get a room full of people talking about how much they hate and have been oppressed by white people, Jews, or blacks, they come out with a hyped generalized hatred for these groups.

White people had safe spaces, too, to openly discuss their "race preservation" and freely express their ideas on other races. It was called the Ku Klux Klan. When you segregate people into groups based on the group's characteristics and exclude anyone that does not share that group identity, it creates a tribalism effect. Tribalism is defined by the behaviors, attitudes, and loyalty that come from belonging to one's own tribe or social group. It is a primitive construct that causes clashes, especially among those who do not "belong" to the tribes. Universities are assisting in what I have previously called the "provide for a divide," in which they actively promote groups to be at odds with each other through campus-promoted outlets. These activities are having lasting impacts on students who take that tribalism mentality out of the university into the real world, and that has helped influence the strong divide we see in the political climate today.

THE PROFESSOR

If you have never had the pleasure of watching the terrible 1998 horror film called "The Faculty," I recommend it if you are looking to watch something dumb yet entertaining. The premise is simple: teachers and administrators at a local high school become controlled by alien parasites that try to infect the students one by one. The movie even contains Jon Stewart, Elijah Wood and Usher, if you are really into those people. Students begin to fight back against the teachers' persuasive measures to try to infect them and take over the student population and then the world. You can see where I'm going with this. University college professors have become a real-life 90s horror movie. Their attempts to infect one student at a time have flourished in a community these parasites thrive in. Some professors try to infect students by advocating the death of people whom they disagree with. Johnny Eric Williams of Trinity College did exactly this by endorsing an article that advocated for first responders to let a group of congressional Republicans die after they were victims of a shooting while practicing for an annual baseball game between the two parties of Congress. Professor Williams shared this story, titled, "Let Them Fucking Die" via Facebook.[20] The article condemns the first responders at the scene who helped save many more lives by taking out the gunman and concludes with this great literature:

> "If you see them drowning. If you see them in a burning building. If they are teetering on the edge of a cliff. If their ships are sinking. If their planes are crashing. If their cars are skidding. If they are overdosing. If their hearts have tellingly arrested. If they are choking in a restaurant. If they are bleeding out in an emergency room. If the ground is crumbling beneath them. If they are in a park and they turn their weapons on each other: Do nothing. *'If you seen them walking down the street and they start to cry, each time you meet, walk on by.'* Least of all, put your life on the line for theirs, and do not dare think doing so, putting your life on the line for theirs, gives you reason or cause to feel celestial. Saving the life of those that would kill you is the opposite of virtuous. Let. Them. Fucking. Die. And smile a bit when you do. For you have done the universe a great service. Ashes to ashes. Dust to bigots."[21]

That is a piece of writing that resonates with Professor Williams. This is a professor who is teaching the kids of today and leaders of tomorrow. That is in our university system. Williams went on to post,

"It is past time for the racially oppressed to do what people who believe themselves to be 'white' will not do, put end to the vectors of their destructive mythology of whiteness and their white supremacy system. #LetThemFuckingDie."

Turns out there are a few professors who just do not like white people. George Ciccariello-Maher was a Drexel University professor who, in December of 2017, posted on Twitter, "All I Want for Christmas is White Genocide." Ciccariello-Maher would eventually resign after ongoing negative backlash to his comment.

A Rutgers University professor used Facebook to go on a rant against white people by posting the following: "OK, officially, I now hate white people. I am a white people, for God's sake, but can we keep them—us—us out of my neighborhood? I just went to Harlem Shake on 124 and Lenox for a Classic burger to go, that would [be] my dinner, and the place is overrun with little Caucasian assholes who know their parents will approve of anything they do. Slide around the floor, you little shithead, sing loudly, you unlikely moron. Do what you want, nobody here is gonna restrict your right to be white. I hereby resign from my race. Fuck these people. Yeah, I know, it's about access to my dinner. Fuck you, too."[22] This post was full of racist remarks and terrible grammar for a university professor.

Then there is the infamous professor at Fresno State, Randa Jarrar. She is best known for her post on Twitter following the death of Barbara Bush. Jarrar posted, "Barbara Bush was a generous and smart and amazing racist who, along with her husband, raised a war criminal. Fuck outa here with your nice words."[23] Jarrar went on to defend her comment with a cringe-worthy post that is both a true and sickening reality of many parasitic professors out there. She stated in another post, "I work as a tenured professor. I make 100K a year doing that. I will never be fired. I will always have people wanting to hear what

I have to say."[24] Craig Bernthal, a professor in Fresno State's English department, agreed with that statement wholeheartedly. "It's easy to be a radical if you're a tenured professor," Bernthal said.

Professors are using universities to express radical viewpoints on a platform that carries a large influence. Some do it to students who unknowingly participate. A professor at Broward College in Fort Lauderdale painted an American flag white, cut it in half and then placed it as a doormat in a high traffic area on campus. The professor, Lisa Rockford, pointed a camera at their feet as students unknowingly walked on it. Broward defended Rockford as this action was meant for an "art project," though many are lost on what exactly was the point that "art" was trying to make.

What is the university's role in ideological diversity? Should they even have one? The growing gap between liberal and conservative professors continues to be a concern when students are being inundated with just one point of view. There should not be an active outcry to fire professors who are liberal and radical. There should be a demand for a more balanced approach. For every "White Racism" class, such as the one instituted at Florida Gulf Coast University, there should be a class on individualism. For every "Racial Capitalism" course offered by Williams College in 2017, which looks at "the ways in which capitalist economies have 'always and everywhere' relied upon forms of racist domination and exclusion," there should be a class on how capitalism has pulled more people out of poverty than any other system. We do not need to advocate for the abolishment of one stance in replacement of another. Professors need to be challenged as well as students. They are part of the problem that is less prone to a solution. Students are their subjects, classrooms are their platform, and their beliefs are tools of influence.

CONCLUSION

There needs to be a balance somewhere in dumb education. There needs to be a method to promote different ideas, not just different skin color. We are conditioning children early and often to one single mind-set. It has caused one group to remain silent on campus while the other group banishes or hides from conflicting ideas. Dumb education has been using the "provide for a divide" method to separate our youth into tribal groups that have developed into real-life consequences of hatred. There are only so many times you can be told whites are racist before you actually start to believe it, even when the thought has never occurred to you. There are only so many times you can be told you are privileged before that guilt starts to creep in, whether or not it is true. We do not need a nation divided after many years of progress.

CHAPTER 6—DUMB CULTURE

As I've stated before, it is very easy to be a liberal in society. Your ideologies are heavily supported and protected in media, Hollywood, entertainment, high schools, universities, and businesses. Your realm of thinking is hardly challenged and, when it is, you have the backing of an entire culture. There is a complete monopoly over culture and it experiences only minor rifts or challenges in the status quo. It is a dumb culture. It is why many believe conservatism is the new counter culture. Back in the 1960s, it was a time for anti-establishment and counter-cultural activism. This revolution brought on many new waves of ideas in alternative lifestyles, race, liberties, rights, anti-war sentiment, environmentalism, free speech, and feminism. Some of it was better, some not so much. The civil rights movement of the 1960s brought on many constitutional liberties that were long overdue for black Americans, including the fight against racial segregation.

But for every civil rights movement, there was a Bill Ayers and his disciples. Ayers is known for his radical ideologies and violent activism. Ayers co-founded the Weather Underground, a communist militant group that was responsible for 25 bombings on places such as the U.S. Capitol, the Pentagon, New York police station, and California Attorney General's office. A bomb accidentally went off during its construction and killed three of his colleagues, including his girlfriend. This explosive was designed to be a nail bomb, meaning its purpose was to kill and hurt as many people as possible. Even Ayers himself verified that it was meant to do serious damage by "tearing through windows and walls and, yes, people, too."[1] Bill Ayers went on to do things such as teach at the University of Illinois-Chicago and host campaign parties at his house for then-Illinois state senate candidate Barack Obama after years of being part of an organization that has been labeled by the FBI as a domestic terrorist group. Only in a dumb culture can a man like this end up teaching college students and fundraising for Democratic party members.

The 1960s were filled with varying degrees of radicalism that spurred what was described as the "New Left"—the progressive counter culture to both Democrats and Republicans. Other revolutionaries of the "New Left" included people such as Joanne Chesimard, who was a member of the Black Panther party and then later the Black Liberation Army. Chesimard is now on the FBI's most wanted list for several felonies including robbery, assault, and taking part in an execution-style murder of a police officer. After her escape from prison, she fled to Cuba where she lives in exile with a $1,000,000 award on her head for info that leads directly to her whereabouts.[2] As of 2018, she is apparently still alive, so there is still a chance to collect!

Then there are those who are less violent yet just as ideologically radical, such as Saul Alinsky. Alinsky is known for his book, "Rules for Radicals," which whom he may not have dedicated directly to but at least acknowledged Lucifer as "the very first radical" who "rebelled against the establishment and did so effectively that he at least won his own kingdom."[3] Take that as seriously as you want, but the fact is that Alinsky was a radical who used mob tactics to promote an "up-against-the-wall" method of "community organization." Alinsky was the topic of Hillary Clinton's college thesis, and Alinsky went so far as to offer her a job.

While Clinton may not have supported all of Alinsky's ideas, she was certainly influenced by them. The point is that activists of the past became the politicians, professors, and businessmen and women of the future. The anti-establishment of the "New Left" became the establishment. They helped frame what has now become the mainstream. They helped frame what is now the existing culture. Think of all the politicians who grew up as young adults in the 1960s during this movement: Maxine Waters, Chuck Schumer, Elizabeth Warren, Bernie Sanders, Bill Clinton, Hillary Clinton, Joe Biden, and many more—all prominent members of the Democratic Party and all part of the establishment today. Their agenda is reiterated in many of the major outlets that have the biggest platforms to help preserve a new culture. The culture war was fought and won by a single idea and it set up major barriers of entry.

HOLLYWOOD

Conservative silence is the worst enemy in culture. However, it has been absolutely necessary for those who want to remained employed and relevant, especially in pop culture. In response to the government shutdown in 2013, when the National Mall allowed a pro-illegal immigration rally to take place, causing vets to struggle to access the WWII memorial, two-time Academy Award-nominated actor James Woods tweeted out against the Barack Obama administration, saying, "This president is a true abomination, to have barricaded the WWII vets but allow illegal aliens privilege." The real news happened when a follower responded to the tweet asking "dude, aren't u worried about...u know... ever working again??" Wood's response was "I don't expect to work again. I think Barack Obama is a threat to the integrity and future of the Republic. My country first."[4]

Since then, Woods has been a vocal supporter of conservative politics, despite being aware of its employment suicide. On July 4, 2018 Woods shared an email from his agent saying, "It's the 4th of July and I'm feeling patriotic. I don't want to represent you anymore. I mean I could go on a rant but you know what I'd say." Woods respectfully responded with, "Dear Ken, I don't actually. I was thinking if you're feeling patriotic, you would appreciate free speech and one's right to think as an individual. Be that as it may, I want to thank you for all your hard work and devotion on my behalf. Be well."

Here is the exact problem. It is not that Hollywood is liberal. Everyone knows that and there are some remarkably talented actors who are devout liberals. The problem is when actors are punished for expressing ideas that do not conform to the rest of Hollywood. This should not be accepted in any type of business. Yet, because of a dumb culture, it has been a recognizable and accepted practice in Hollywood.

Intimidating those who are different than us was a principle that was hard fought against in America. Yet, we throw that out the window because look, an explosion there or a pretty actress over here or look, so and so actress had a nip slip. This is an industry that is always spouting off about diversity as if it is an Ivy League school admissions department. In 2016, many major players in Hollywood boycotted or spoke heavily against the 2016 Oscar Awards because all actors for the four major acting categories were white. This includes the elites such as Will Smith, George Clooney, Cuba Gooding, Jr. and Spike Lee.

At least actor Idris Elba spoke a little differently on diversity when addressing the British Parliament. Elba stated the following: "I'm not here to talk about black people. I'm here to talk about diversity. Diversity in the modern world is more than just skin color. It's gender, age, disability, sexual orientation, social background and—most important of all, as far as I'm concerned—diversity of thought."[5] Idris Elba is right in this regard. There is no inclusion in Hollywood. It is straight exclusion.

Even actor Tim Allen was asked on the Jimmy Kimmel show about going to the Donald Trump presidential inauguration. After stuttering around the question, Allen finally said yes. When Jimmy Kimmel noticed Allen stumbling on the question, he reassured him he was not "attacking" him with the question. This lead to Allen saying, "I'm not kidding, you gotta be real careful around here. You get beat up if you don't believe what everybody believes; it's like '30s Germany." This begs the question that, if Hollywood is so inclusive, why would this not be a concerning issue to them? This is why Olympic gold medalist and reality TV star Caitlyn Jenner, formally known as Bruce Jenner, said it was easy to come out as trans but harder to come out as a Republican.

It is a popular consensus that you will have consequences coming out as a Republican in Hollywood. If actors are scared to come out about their sexuality because they fear their career would be in danger, then there would be a public uproar, complete with a hashtag movement. Rightfully so, too. Would Hollywood outcast actors because they have a different sexual orientation? Absolutely not. Would Hollywood actively keep people out of the business because they have a different skin color? Nope. But what Hollywood will do is keep you out of the business if you do not belong to its group think. That is what makes Hollywood part of the dumb culture.

After the 2016 election that resulted in a Donald Trump victory, it did not take long for celebrities to have an absolute meltdown. Considerably so, since a lot of celebrities were donors to the Hillary Clinton campaign. Jeffrey Katzenberg, CEO of DreamWorks Animation, donated $1 million to Priorities USA Action, one of the largest Democratic Party super PACs that backed Clinton in 2016. Steven Spielberg donated $1 million to this PAC as well. Director and producer J.J. Abrams shelled out $502,700 to Priorities USA Action and the Clinton campaign. There were plenty of A-list celebrities that gave the maximum individual donation campaign amount, which is set at $2,700, directly to Hillary Clinton's campaign. Some of these reported contributors include Leonardo DiCaprio, Ben Affleck, Reese Witherspoon, Barbra Streisand, Quincy Jones, Katy Perry, Seth MacFarlane, Kate Hudson, Beyoncé, Bryan Cranston, Elizabeth Banks, Sarah Silverman, Richard Gere, Tobey Maguire, Jesse Eisenberg, Rob Reiner, and Ellen DeGeneres. There are many celebrities that made vocal endorsements to Democrats and Hillary, but the combined net worth of these aforementioned celebrities is $7.5 billion.[6] These stars have power and relevancy and, most important, not just a platform but THE platform. A total of $84 million was made in campaign contributions from individuals and firms in television, movies, and music in the 2016 election cycle, with 80 percent going to Democrats.[7]

The Democratic Party has some of the biggest players in Hollywood firmly in its pocket. During the 2016 campaign, an ensemble of actors made a video designed to encourage people to vote. The ad featured heavy hitters such as Robert Downey, Jr., Scarlett Johansson, Neil Patrick Harris, Keegan-Michael Key, James Franco, Martin Sheen, Leslie Odom Jr., Don Cheadle, and Mark Ruffalo. The ad tried its best to just be a subjective promotion on voting, but its bias could not be contained. While it never once mentioned Clinton or Trump, it made enough innuendos to know exactly who you should support because big-time celebrities were telling you to. The ad goes on to say, "You only get this many famous people together if the issue is one that truly matters to all of us." Meaning you should really pay attention because overpaid celebrities are telling you to. "A disease or an ecological crisis or a racist, abusive coward who could permanently damage the fabric of our society. Do the math. Do we really wanna give nuclear weapons to a man whose signature move is firing things?" If I had to guess, I would think that comment was more directed to Donald Trump, considering his signature phrase was "you're fired" on the show The Apprentice.

The rhetoric does not stop there, with continuing phrases like, "We cannot pretend both sides are equally unfavorable" and "this election will affect everything from 'immigration' to 'common sense gun laws,'" and that your vote will "protect this country from fear and ignorance." This video has been viewed more than 8.5 million times on YouTube. Other celebrities tried finding more creative and inspiring ways to get the public out to vote for Hillary. Madonna told a crowd at Madison Square Garden that, "If you vote for Hillary Clinton, I will give you a blow job," the has-been pop singer stated. "Okay? I'm really good. I'm not a douche and I'm not a tool. I take my time, I have a lot of eye contact, and I do swallow," she bragged.[8] I do not imagine that promise was fulfilled, but it is Madonna, after all, so who knows?

It is no wonder there was a massive meltdown from celebrities after their shoe-in candidate lost the election despite all their money, publicity, oral sex promises, and ad campaigns failed them miscrably. In fact, many celebrities said they would move out of the United States if Trump won.

Here is yet another list of left-leaning elites; this time they were ones who made these empty threats:

Samuel L. Jackson—He stated that if that "motherfucker" (Trump) won he would move his "black ass to South Africa."[9] While this was mostly stated as a joke from Jackson, it was meant to pander to an audience that resonates with the idea that moving out of the country is the only solution to a Trump presidential victory.

Chelsea Handler—Handler said she would have a house in Spain that will be ready for her right after the election. On "Live With Kelly and Michael," she reiterated this point by saying, "I did buy a house in another country just in case, so all of these people that threaten to leave the country and then don't, I will leave the country."[10] Of course, what instead happened was she cried on camera during a show and backed out of her plan.

Lena Dunham—At the Matrix Awards, Dunham stated, "I know a lot of people have been threatening to do this, but I really will," echoing a similar statement made by Chelsea Handler. "I know a lovely place in Vancouver and I can get my work done from there."[11]

Raven Symonè—She was supposed to have already purchased tickets to Canada where she planned to move with her "entire family" if any Republican candidate became president.[12]

Whoopi Goldberg—Co-host on "The View" during a rant on Trump and immigration stated that, "maybe it's time for me to move, you know," adding that she could "afford to go" if she wanted to.[13]

Miley Cyrus—In a tear-filled selfie on Instagram, Cyrus claimed that her "heart is broken into a 100,000 pieces" after the election of Donald Trump. She concluded her heart-throbbing post by saying, "Honestly fuck this shit I am moving if this is my president! I don't say things I don't mean!"[14]

Amy Schumer—When comedian Amy Schumer was asked if her acts would change if Donald Trump became president, she said, "My acts will change because I will need to learn to speak Spanish because I will move to Spain. Or somewhere." Schumer continued to say that a Trump victory would be "beyond my comprehension" and it is "too crazy."[15]

None of these celebrities actually moved, despite their claims that they "don't say things they don't mean" or they "really will" so you better take them seriously. This is part of a dumb culture where you can say one thing yet, when push comes to shove, the convictions go out the window. It was dumb when Stephen Baldwin said, "I'll be moving out of the country" if Barack Obama won the presidency back in 2008 and it was dumb when it was said by other celebrities in 2016.[16] The question is, have any of these celebrities' lives been worse off since Trump became president? Or when Bush did? The opposite is probably true, considering they have been better off with tax cuts over recent years.

The platforms entertainers have helps promote ideologies to a susceptible audience but it also exploits their hypocrisies. In 2018, rapper Eminem used a performance at the iHeart Radio Music awards to attack the NRA. The verse went like this:

> *"This whole country is going nuts, and the NRA is in our way.*
>
> *They're responsible for this whole production*
>
> *They hold the strings, they control the puppet*
>
> *And they threaten to take donor bucks*
>
> *So they know the government won't do nothing and no one's budging*
>
> *Gun owners clutching their loaded weapons*
>
> *They love their guns more than our children."*

Very insightful and powerful stuff. It even almost made sense. Here is another verse from a popular Eminem titled "Sing for the Moment":

> *"See what these kids do is hear about us totin' pistols*

And they want to get one 'cause they think the shit's cool

Not knowin' we really just protectin' ourselves, we entertainers

Of course the shit's affectin' our sales, you ignoramus. "

This is a guy that was arrested for pistol whipping another man outside of a bar in Michigan. This is a guy who has written songs titled "Kill You," "Gun In Your Grill," and "Pistol Pistol." This is a guy with lyrics such as "the clip slider, love to blast a Mag, you're a fag." This is a guy that is part of a dumb culture.

The NRA promotes gun safety as well as the right of individuals to protect themselves, not senseless violence portrayed through many of Eminem's songs. At the Golden Globes Awards ceremony, actress Connie Britton showed up in a sweater with the words "Poverty is Sexist." While the shirt's message is conflicting, considering there are far more homeless men than women, it should also be noted that it retails for $380. This is an instance where the virtue-signaling on a platform for millions of people to see is more important than the actual substance of doing something.

You may have noticed Alec Baldwin appearing in Capital One commercials recently. What you haven't noticed is that, back in 2008, Alec Baldwin wrote a short piece titled "To Hell with Wall Street" for *The Huffington Post*. Baldwin was against the bailouts of 2008 for financial institutions, such as Capital One, saying, "Don't give them the money. Don't loan it." Yet Baldwin was happy to take money from Capital One to do commercials.

Harrison Ford is the vice chair of Conservation International, which is an organization that states it addresses climate change through mitigation of "working to prevent further climate change by reducing emissions, enhancing carbon storage, etc."[17] In an interview, Ford revealed his love for flying by saying, "I'm so passionate about flying

I often fly up the coast for a cheeseburger."[18] I'm sure those emissions used to get a cheeseburger are completely justifiable to a man who sits as vice chair to an organization against increased CO2 emissions.

Famous rapper Jay-Z has called out President Trump's comments as "disappointing and hurtful" about Haiti and other places being part of "shithole countries." This is a guy who has lyrics that state, "You know I thug em, fuck em, love em, leave em, cause I don't fuckin need em." While Trump is known to say some pretty dumb things, Jay-Z is a guy that is part of a rap culture that is heavily misogynistic and promotes violence and drug use. But he is a celebrity and, at least at this moment, is married to Beyoncé, so Americans tend to believe there is more merit to what ridiculously wealthy entertainers have to say solely because they are famous.

No matter how hypocritical, this is the business that has the biggest outlets. They do not like outsiders invading their space. This is why Kanye West's support for Donald Trump made headlines in 2018. West stated his support for Trump on twitter by posting "We are both dragon energy. He is my brother. I love everyone. I don't agree with everything anyone does. That's what makes us individuals. And we have the right to independent thought." West is spot on with the individualist attitude, even if it had not been specific to Trump. Predictably, the rest of Hollywood did not take to kindly to it. Snoop Dogg responded to West's support by using Instagram to say that is "mighty white of u Kanye." Rosie O'Donnell replied to his tweet saying, "[Trump's] a fucking moron kanye – wake up from the illusion."[19] Singer and songwriter Moby responded by tweeting, "Come on, Kanye, you're too smart and talented to be a [Donald Trump] supporter. [Trump] is a racist and a sociopath who is ruining the country the same way he ruined most of his businesses."

If anyone in the celebrity world tweets, posts or publicly states anything positive on Democratic candidates, it does not make any news. It happens in abundance. Eventually, no one cares or pays any attention to it because it is part of the cultural norm that they are supposed to fit in. This is why Tina Fey can stereotype women while at the same time advocating as a feminist. We saw this when she said this about the 2016 election: "A lot of this election was turned by white, college-educated women who now would maybe like to forget about this election and go back to watching HGTV."[19] I guess all white women with college degrees stay at home and watch HGTV? At least she did not say Lifetime because that would have been sexist.

Hollywood will continue to promote its propaganda through television, movies, theater, music, and entertainment. Again, this is not a call to swing the ideological pendulum in a whole other direction. It is to try to find a balance where actors do not get chastised out of work for their political views—a balance where, if you want to rap about obscene material, then do it but leave out the hypocritical virtue signaling when someone says something you disagree with. At the very least, this should be an industry that does not shun half its audience and blatantly try to conform to the other half.

MEDIA

Media helps define a culture and can shape a narrative to a degree of perception. Today, there are more outlets of media than ever before that have become even more intimate with popular culture, as culture and media depend on each other. Media does not just promote news or stories but promotes ideas, feelings, moods, and attitudes. It lets us know what is important and what is not. It is a communication network designed to report on the culture as well as help define it. The class-dominant theory of media suggests that media portrays the views of an elite minority that controls the media outlets. This means that these elite can control what people see and, more important, what they do not see. For example, if a media conglomerate supports a particular candidate, it is less likely to negatively report on that candidate. While these elite can be corporate in nature, such as having a large advertiser on a news program, that news outlet is less likely to negatively report on that company.

Turner Broadcasting Systems, Inc. is one of America's largest media conglomerates. They own and operate some of the largest brands in entertainments including: CNN, TBS, TNT, Bleacher Report, truTV, HLN, Adult Swim, and others. Turner Broadcasting System Founder Ted Turner has always been a supporter of the Democratic Party. It goes all the way back to 1992 when Larry King was caught on a hot mic telling Bill Clinton, "Ted Turner changed the world. He's a big fan of yours. He would serve you, you know what I mean? He's ready, what's he got left in life to gain. I'd call him after you're elected. Think about it."[20] When Hillary Clinton showed signs of a health condition in 2016, which was used by Trump as a tool during the election to say she was physically unfit to be president, Dr. Drew Plinksy of the HLN show, "Dr. Drew on Call," echoed the statement, saying he was "gravely concerned not just about [Clinton's] health, but her health care."[21] No specific statement was made on why his show was canceled, but the timing of the cancellation was suspicious, given the fact that it happened only a week after he made those comments. HLN is part of the Turner Broadcasting System. Ted Turner made his endorsement of Clinton public in 2016 by saying in an email that she has the leadership skills and best qualifications to become president.[22]

Though Turner has sold off Turner Broadcasting System to Time Warner (now Warner Media), the brands remained loyal to their bias. TBS airs Samantha Bee's late-night talk show "Full Frontal with Samantha Bee." Bee has been a staunch critic of Trump and the Republican Party, and even went so far as to call Donald Trump's daughter Ivanka a "feckless cunt" during a rant about immigration.[23]

Then there is CNN, and no one can deny its political bias unless they are blissfully ignorant to that fact. Jeff Zucker, the president of CNN, has overseen a failing network that has been rife with unreliable, biased reporting that even led to the resignation of three journalists in 2017. CNN has continued to fall in last place behind other major networks in terms of viewership ratings. It is a good thing so many airports at least run CNN's programs so they remain somewhat relevant. Zucker is an outspoken Democratic supporter and has even said, "I think it was a legitimate criticism of CNN that it was a little too liberal."[24] This is no surprise, given that CNN is a product of Turner Broadcasting System, which is owned by Time Warner/Warner Communications. Considering that Time Warner donated over $400,000 to Hillary Clinton's campaigns, it makes a lot of sense.[25]

Warner Media also controls Warner Brothers and HBO. HBO is known for its liberal agenda through the promotion of its talk shows, "Last Week Tonight with John Oliver" and the long standing "Real Time with Bill Maher."

A piece titled, "How Comcast Bought the Democratic Party," by the National Review, highlights the connections of this media conglomerate with Democrats. Brian L. Roberts has contributed large amounts of money to many Democratic figures such as Barack Obama, Bob Casey, Kristen Gillibrand, and Steny Hoyer. Senior Executive Vice President and Chief Diversity Officer David L. Cohen is no different. Cohen served as chief of staff to Democratic mayor of Philadelphia, Edward Rendell. According to the article, Cohen raised more than $2 million for Obama and visited the White House 14 times.[26] This is significant because Comcast is just another conglomerate that owns

NBCUniversal Media. NBCUniversal owns and operates MSNBC, CNBC, the Golf Channel, E!, Universal Studios, and USA Network.

The Pew Research Center found that MSNBC news contains 85 percent opinion and only 15 percent news. MSNBC is widely considered the most liberal news program, which is fine, considering they do not try to hide or cover their biased opinions. No one would argue that Rachel Maddow, who fought back tears on air after the 2016 Trump victory, is a political independent. In her defense, she was not the only grown-up to be flooded with overwhelming emotion on MSNBC over the election. MSNBC's Lawrence O'Donnell offered his sentiments after the election by saying, "America is crying tonight. I'm not sure how much of America, but a very, very significant portion and I mean literally crying." Mika Brzenzinski of MSNBC's show "Morning Joe" said that "everybody is crying and so upset and it is the end of their world." I can say for a definitive fact that not everybody cried and the end of the world has yet to come.

In 2018, a "Media Bias Chart" was created by patent attorney Vanessa Otero to show the different levels of bias and reliability of news outlets. The chart gained a lot of attention and it is widely used and debated today. It has been modified many times since its original back in 2016 because it has contained a little bit of bias itself. Nevertheless, out of the major cable news outlets—CNN, MSNBC, NBC, and ABC—were all considered, at the very least, liberal leaning. Not only did the cable news outlets dominate the liberal side, but major publications and outlets such as *The New York Times*, *Washington Post*, NPR, Vox, *Vanity Fair*, BBC, AP and others lean heavily left—all major outlets, all liberal-biased.

The only major cable news show on the chart that was considered conservative was Fox News. Not only were they considered conservative, they are apparently "Hyper-Partisan Conservative" and "Nonsense damaging to public discourse."[27] This is an example of why the chart itself may contain some bias. Despite that, this chart only proves everything everyone already knows, recognizes, expects, and accepts from the mainstream media, which is that there is a thought-dominated monopoly on media that is helping shape our culture. This is why Fox News dominates in viewership ratings over and over again. There is no other option. They have no other competition in cable news. All other outlets are a controlled narrative. If you are a conservative and want to watch a program that panders to your thinking, Fox News is all you've got. For 16 years, the Fox News Channel has been rated as the top cable news channel in both daytime and prime-time viewing, according to Nielsen Media Research numbers.[28]

Media bias, though recognized, is mostly unchecked. This is what led to a colossal failure among journalists who were certain in their predictions that Hillary Clinton would run away with the 2016 presidential election. Their bubble is impenetrable because they live in a world with no sharp objects. The bias is not just recognized, but it is supported by facts to help those who still struggle with the idea that journalism is not a level playing field. *Politico* researched geographic relevance to where most internet publishing has taken place over the last few years. It comes as no surprise that nearly 90 percent of all internet publishing employees work in a county that Clinton won during the 2016 presidential election. Seventy-five percent of employees work in a county that Clinton won by 30 percentage points. The question is not if these journalists are affected by their environment, but to what degree they are affected. We are all shaped by the environment we live in, whether it is the household we grew up in, the university we attended, the city we were born in, or the state we live in.

Even if these employees do not let the effects of their surroundings come out in publishing, which it typically does, it can still be used as a tool of influence. For example, it is easy to dissuade voters if you have a platform that is used to constantly tell those voters that their candidate does not have a chance and they should stay at home on election night. It is not just the counties that journalists live in that determines their bias. It is the fact that so few actually identify as Republicans. Indiana professors Lars Willnat and David H. Weaver conducted an online study of 1,080 reporters to find exactly how few of them were Republican. Though this study was conducted in 2013, it notes that a meager 7.1 percent identified as Republicans. In this study, 28.1 percent identified as Democrats, 50.2 percent identified as Independents, and 14.6 percent described their affiliations as "other." The numbers are there, the proof is in the coverage, and there is still a strong denial of media bias that has been chalked up as a right-wing conspiracy. It is hard to take the media seriously when it is the same one that says that the Obama administration was "virtually scandal-free," which is exactly what MSNBC's Mike Barnicle said when comparing the Trump and Obama presidencies. Barnicle is quick to forget an IRS scandal that specifically targeted pro-conservative organizations that sought to acquire tax-exempt status. Or that the Justice Department armed cartel members through a gunrunning operation known as "Fast and Furious" that led to the murder of an American citizen. Or when the administration tried to blame an irrelevant YouTube video for the death of Ambassador Chris Stevens and three others in Benghazi. The list of Obama scandals could go on, but the point is that the media protects their own. To pretend the media bubble does not exist is at the very least ignorant and at the most just outright dumb politics. These are journalists who live in Democratic counties, identify as Democrats, and protect Democrats.

The bias and, most important, the class dominance of media has led to an all-time high in distrust of the news. A survey done by Axios in 2018 found that 92 percent of Republicans think the media reports news they know to be, false or purposely, misleading.[29] It is fair for Republicans to be more skeptical, considering most of the mainstream media is inherently in the pocket of one party and it certainly is not the Republicans. However, even 53 percent of Democrats think media is intentionally reporting fake news. Seventy-nine percent of independents also believe this to be true.

There is some good news among millennials and their trust for the media. In fact, millennials do not trust anyone. The Harvard University's Institute of Politics surveyed 3,034 18- to 29-year-olds and found that 88 percent of millennials say they only "sometimes" or "never" trust the press.[30] So, while it is true across the political spectrum, it is common in millennials, too. They also do not trust government (74 percent), Congress (82 percent) or even the Supreme Court (58 percent). There are many other studies done around the level of trust about the media and they all have ended up with the same or similar conclusions: no one trusts them anymore. It is like asking if you won a date with Harvey Weinstein, would you go? The answer is always no because you can never trust the outcome or the intentions.

This is the same media that was exposed when emails from the Hillary Clinton campaign were leaked, revealing a distinguished list of journalists and news anchors invited to join the campaign with the goal of "framing the HRC [Hillary Rodham Clinton] message and framing the race."[31] Let that sink in just a bit. Journalists were invited to an "off-the-record" dinner to help "frame" the message. Pundits like to discuss the Trump-Russia alleged collusion, but what the dumb culture ignores is that there was an active collusion with the Clinton campaign and big media to deceive the American public. This invite was sent in 2015 before Clinton even announced her campaign bid. Notable members invited on that list include the following:

George Stephanopoulos – ABC	Jackie Kucinich – Daily Beast	Ryan Lizza – New Yorker
Diane Sawyer – ABC	Whitney Snyder– Huffington Post	Jonathan Martin – NYT
John Heileman - Bloomberg	Alex Wagner – MSNBC	Maggie Haberman – NYT
Mark Halperin - Bloomberg	Beth Fouhy – MSNBC	Sandra Sobieraj Westfall – People
Jeff Zucker – CNN	Phil Griffin – MSNBC	Glenn Thrush – Politico
Jake Taper – CNN	Rachael Maddow – MSNBC	Mike Allen – Politico
David Chalian – CNN	Rachel Racusen – MSNBC	Maria-Elena Salinas - Univision
Mark Preston – CNN	Savannah Guthrie – NBC	Alyssa Mastromonaco – VICE
Sam Feist – CNN	Mike Oreskes - NPR	Jon Allen - VOX

You can see the big names from major outlets that were able to influence the 2016 election. That is just a sample of people on that invitation list. It is a popularity contest. Everyone wants to help shape the culture. This is part of the reason why there is so much distrust. This is what happens when you have large media conglomerates' executives having a top-down political effect on brands. After all, they say that fish rots from the head.

BIG BUSINESS

There was a time when big business was considered to be a tool of the Republican Party. Their influence, donations, and lobbying had ultimate control and sway over representative opinion. Their greed could supposedly only be satisfied by Republicans that advocate for them in Washington. Big business is now a part of our culture, which means they have switched out the puppets.

The Clinton campaign received many large donations from big

business such as DreamWorks, Google, Morgan Stanley, JPMorgan Chase, Time Warner, Salesforce, Corning, Bank of America, Microsoft and DISH Network.[32] This is a party that is supposed to oppose corporations and their "crony capitalism" tactics, yet they take support when it benefits them. And it does benefit them. This is seen even more so in the tech space. 2ndVote is an organization that is stated to be a "conservative watchdog for corporate activism" by scoring companies on a scale from 1 to 5, with 1 being more liberal and 5 being more conservative. A score of 3 means you are not biased to either side. Scores are based on factors such as direct or indirect donations that support liberal groups, causes, and organizations, and vice versa.

Apple received a score of 1 out of 5. That score has a lot to do with their political contributions. The Center for Responsive Politics runs a website called OpenSecrets that describes itself as follows: "Nonpartisan, independent and nonprofit, the Center for Responsive Politics is the nation's premier research group tracking money in U.S. politics and its effect on elections and public policy." This organization reports that Apple gave $653,584 to Hillary Clinton, which was their largest contribution to recipients in 2016. While they gave more to Republicans in the House ($76,015) compared to Democrats ($66,304) this difference was made up by giving $145,528 more to Democrats in the Senate.[33] Facebook also scored a 1 out of 5 by 2ndVote and this can be attributed to many reasons. Since 2014, Democratic Senator Cory Booker has received more in contributions from Facebook than any other senator at $64,825. Democrat Nancy Pelosi has received the most out of all representatives in the House at $50,150.

Facebook has supported members on both sides of the aisle, like most companies, but they lean much more to Democrats. Facebook is a major contributor and influencer of our culture. Much like the media and other social networks, they control, support, and push a single narrative. The difference is that they have that ability more so than anyone previously. Facebook has been routinely called out for censorship of pro-conservative material from flagging posts and banning pro-right pages.

Several former Facebook employees admitted to website Gizmodo that they were instructed to prevent right-wing stories from appearing on the "trending" news section. This section gave users the ability to see what stories were most popular at the time. Not only did they prevent stories from hitting the trending section, they also "injected" selected stories that did not meet the criteria of being in the top trending section.[34] This means Facebook was operating more like a news publication than a social media platform, since they are able to dictate what news and stories their users can see at any time. It was even reported that stories covered by conservative outlets that met the criteria of trending stories were omitted from the list unless a mainstream outlet—such as the *New York Times*, BBC and CNN—covered the same story. If and when one of those mainstream outlets published that story, too, they would substitute the conservative publication with a liberal one.

Censorship by social media platforms is now just part of this dumb culture. A Twitter employee was caught on camera admitting that they used a "shadow ban" technique on conservative accounts, meaning they got banned without even knowing. "I would say the majority of it was for Republicans," Twitter employee Pranay Singh said. This was discovered by James O'Keefe's Project Veritas, which used undercover tactics to show how biased Twitter actually is.[35] One content review agent at Twitter even said, "if it was a pro-Trump thing and I'm anti-Trump... I banned his whole account... it's at your discretion." Both Twitter and Facebook deny doing this "to their knowledge," as any good PR person would advise them to do.

Here is the concern: over 88 percent of 18- to 29-year-olds are reported to use any form of social media.[36] Eighty percent use Facebook while 45 percent use Twitter. In another poll, it showed that 47 percent of adults use social media as a news source.[37] And this is a growing trend. Social media platforms are big business and they have gone the route that our news and media have gone. Culture is their business, not social media, where they can define it the way they want to steer it. Other tech companies such as Microsoft, Amazon and Google scored 1, 1.9, and 1 respectively by 2ndVote.

Eric Schmidt was Google's CEO from 2001 to 2011, then became the executive chairman of Google's parent company, Alphabet. Schmidt was heavily invested in Hillary Clinton's campaign, as seen by the content from hacked emails from John Podesta, a long-time Clinton adviser. A year before announcing the campaign, Podesta wrote this about Google's executive chairman to a campaign manager:

> "He's ready to fund, advise, recruit talent, etc. He was more deferential on structure than I expected. Wasn't pushing to run through one of his existing firms. Clearly wants to be head outside advisor, but didn't seem like he wanted to push others out. Clearly wants to get going. He's still in DC tomorrow and would like to meet with you if you are in DC in the afternoon. I think it's worth doing."[38]

Schmidt invested in a number of start-ups that helped Clinton's 2016 campaign with ways to use data to improve voter turnout and engagement, as well as improve advertising.

Another example can be seen with Reid Hoffman, who is one of the co-founders of LinkedIn and PayPal and an active investor in Silicon Valley. He has donated to the American Civil Liberties Union as well as Win the Future—groups that push Democratic Party causes while being the combatants of the Trump administration. Reid has been willing to spend hundreds of millions of dollars to fund organizations that support the Democratic Party and fight the Trump agenda.[39]

If these examples are not enough, then take a study done by political science professors at Stanford University. Professors David Broockman and Neil Malhotra, with the help of freelance journalist and tech writer Gregory Ferenstein, did a 2017 study titled "Wealthy Elites' Policy Preferences and Economic Inequality: The Case of Technology Entrepreneurs." The goal is to find out how tech elites think and their political motives. The numbers confirm that tech entrepreneurs are, in fact, liberal. In 2016, 75.2 percent voted for Hillary Clinton compared to the 8.8 percent that voted for Donald Trump. And 61.3 percent identified as Democrats, and only 14.1 percent identified as Republicans.

Sure, there is still a good amount of support from businesses to Republicans. After all, if you run a platform of low taxes, less regulation, and growth opportunities, you are going to get business-minded support. Republicans have not denied that. Democrats have opposed big business for that exact reason.

CONCLUSION

We are a society heavily defined by our culture. Changing a culture is something that does not happen overnight. With the powers that be in media, business, Hollywood, and universities, it may never change. In fact, it may just grow stronger. Andrew Breitbart famously noted that "politics is downstream from culture," Breitbart knew this was a battle to be taken seriously. Do not let people on the right downplay anyone in popular culture coming out with pro-conservative views. It is important not to control the culture but to at least make an attempt to balance it out, and that starts with people starting to speak up about their convictions.

"There is an underground conservative movement," Breitbart said in 2009. "I have more friends who are conservative in [Hollywood], with brand names, writers, directors, graphic artists, comedians, singers, song writers, rock and rollers, punk rockers, believe it or not, who love this country, most of whom are cultural conservatives, and who have existed in the closet for the last 40 years, because the conservative movement was, for the most part, based in the Northeast and kind of pooh-poohed the culture or just didn't think that there was a cultural right out there."[40]

The New Left of the 1960s became the new culture. They are dominant in this space today which, in effect, cannot make these principles the counter culture if they are mainstream. People will argue against this notion by stating that the Republicans control a majority of the Senate, Congress and the Presidency. But this controls changes in just about every election cycle. When the culture shifted in the 1960s, it was controlled by JFK and Lyndon Johnson, with Democratic control in both the House and Senate. In fact, Democrats controlled the House and Senate from 1955-1979. Thus it was termed the "New Left" movement. YouTube personality and political commentator Paul Joseph Watson brought popularity to this counter-culture idea. It was met by criticism by those on the left pointing out that social justice warriors have an established work of controversial tactics and this by definition is counter culture.

An example is Colin Kaepernick taking a knee during the national anthem. People said this kept Kaepernick from being signed by NFL owners. Those same people probably did not realize that it may have been because he just was not that good. They tend to forget about the amount of high profile, and even low profile, football players that also took knees during the anthem but remained employed throughout 2017. Hell, some teams did not even come out of the locker room during the national anthem.

Another controversial jaunt was when comedian Kathy Griffin posted a picture of herself holding a life-like, decapitated, blood-smeared head of Donald Trump but claimed it as art. Nonetheless, she issued an apology and everything was back to normal for this D-list performer. But when a simple act of coming out as a conservative or having support for Donald Trump incites heavy public and professional scrutiny, there is obviously an established culture. Anything that upsets that culture is met with swift repercussions, even if it is not even remotely controversial.

CHAPTER 7—DUMB CONCLUSION

Dumb politics is not always rooted in some kind of malicious intent. In fact, for the most part it is quite the opposite. Dumb politics is often done with the best intentions. Yet, no matter how good the intentions are, nothing is solved when one group benefits at the expense of another. Too often our political climate is geared by emotion. It is the bleeding heart reaction that can end up doing more bad than good. Not everyone can or will ever be pleased. Moving away from this line of thinking will open up the ability to think cognitively about how we can create an environment of opportunity rather than foster an environment of dependency.

No one is more susceptible to dumb politics than the politicians themselves. Politicians are a ship without an anchor being pushed in the direction of whatever new wave of progressivism is currently leading the tide. Too often, it is the naivety of the young making the biggest splash that catches the eye of politicians. But this is nothing groundbreaking. Instead, it is a new youth with the same message and, with each generation, the youth always believe they are onto something revolutionary. Nothing is revolutionary when they assimilate with the masses of today, yesterday, and the future. They become part of the dumb politics that is rooted in immigration, economics, education, and culture.

Dumb Politics mistakes envy for empathy. This coins terms and slogans that bleed with empathy, such as the term "living wage," as if the opposite to a living wage is a death wage and any support outside of that living wage implies that a person who does not support a living wage supports killing people through low wages. Only a living wage can keep you alive, and that is where many are fooled to believe this is all an act of empathy.

But what is empathetic about business owners having to close their businesses because they are forced to pay wages they cannot afford? What is empathetic about pricing low-skilled and inexperienced workers out of a job? Redistribution polices are not empathetic. The moral high ground of a progressive collectivism mentality is a hole in the ground, not a virtuous mountain top. There are unintended consequences for every policy that is mistakenly called empathetic.

There is a reason this book's title does not specify the ignorance of a millennial generation. Dumb politics did not form just in this last generation. That ignorance has been passed down from past generations. It has only strengthened and been promoted by those who let that ignorance become part of our everyday political climate. Now that ignorance is being voted on, it is gaining ground because now politicians can take advantage of a susceptible group that has voting power. Politicians will never underestimate the ignorance of the masses and will, instead, use it to their advantage.

Covering everything in dumb politics would be an exhausting process. There is an overwhelming abundance of dumb politics in the areas presented in this book, and there are many topics that have not been covered. Since it has been reported that 74 percent of millennials have taken Adderall and 82 percent have used it in college to help study and keep the many distractions surrounding us at bay, it is imperative to keep it short and to the point. I know my audience, mostly because I am part of that audience and a generation of ADD. That being said, it is important to look back and reflect on all the main topics presented as well as the key take-aways.

DUMB NAME CALLING

- Labeling people with hateful rhetoric does not further a political discussion. We have been inundated with attacking to get the biggest reaction out of the other side instead of trying to articulate a position.

- Fascism is one of the most common terms used on conservatives and Republican leaders. Yet few know the true definition of fascism. Fascism eliminates a key component of conservativism—individualism. In a fascist state, all contribute to the betterment of the community before the individual. Fascism is anti-capitalism, where government controls the means of distribution and creates a corporatism of business and government. Fascism would be a favored system among many socialists if it were not for the Social Darwinism aspect that acts as a means of race preservation

- Groups such as Antifa use fascist tactics to violently bully and intimidate opposing views of their organization. It is disguised as a way to protect against racism and bigotry, but has no method to validate any of these claims they use against opponents. Simply put, if you are a conservative, you are a target.

- Racism is not defined to be specific to one group. Any race can experience racism from any other race that imposes it.

DUMB IMMIGRATION

- Yes, we are a nation of immigrants. Native Americans arrived here thousands of years ago. Then our Founding Fathers arrived. Many more immigrants followed and some, unfortunately, arrived against their will. None of that matters when it comes to establishing our immigration standards today. We have the right as a sovereign nation to decide who comes in and who stays out. It is the law. The same reasons why universities have standards for acceptance can be mirrored in our nation. We want to preserve a certain level of prestige when it comes to our nation. That is not to say we do not want any immigrants. Don't let dumb immigration tell you otherwise.

- Politicians want to lecture us on immigration when 77 percent of our representatives do not even represent bordering states with Mexico and some take residency in 96 percent white states.

- Sensible border security discussion used to not matter what party you belonged to. Bill Clinton had a strong stance on border security. Barack Obama, although he did not speak too often about it, had excessive deportation numbers.

- The violence in Mexico has become an absolute epidemic. There were 29,168 murders in 2017, a 27 percent increase from 2016.

- Texas shares 1,254 miles of the 1,900 miles of border between the U.S. and Mexico. It is hard for the rest of the country to sympathize with border security since the problem is simply passed to bordering states

- Drugs are flooding our borders and stimulating the growth and power of cartels. The U.S. Border Patrol seized 15,182 pounds of heroin, 10,273 pounds of methamphetamine, 6,174 pounds of cocaine and 857,888 pounds of marijuana in 2017 at the border sectors of Mexico.

- Illegal immigration is a burden on the tax payer. The cost of illegal immigration is $116 billion for U.S. tax payers.

- Money is leaving the U.S. to benefit Mexico. In 2017, $26.1 billion in remittances was sent across the border.

- U.S. workers are feeling the pain. A saturation in the market of illegal workers leads to decreasing wages for those in that particular sector.

- Mexico has its share of harsh immigration policies, especially as it is measured against the United States.

- Millennials are not in favor of more border security. Only 23 percent of African-American, 22 percent of Asian-American, 15 percent of Latinx, and 40 percent of White millennials support building a wall to stop illegal immigration.

DUMB ECONOMICS

- Economic policies need to be examined in the long term as well as foreseeing consequences beyond first and second parties.

- Raising the minimum wage is a great platform for politicians to use on blissfully ignorant voters who do not see the already realized unintended consequences of these artificial wage increases. Corporations have the capital and resources to absorb a mandatory increase of the minimum wage. It is small businesses that are closing their doors for good in areas where the minimum wage was increased to $15 per hour. If there is no additional output from employees to justify raising wages, both employee and employer suffer negative consequences.

- Scandinavian countries are always a popular reference for proponents of socialism. Yet these countries practice what is described as the "Nordic Model," which has free market principles but high rates of taxation. These high tax rates have stifled a lot of the growth and innovation these countries used to enjoy.

- Millennials support socialism. Polls have shown that 58 percent of millennials favor either socialism, communism, or fascism over capitalism.

- Tax cuts can lead to higher tax revenue, as demonstrated by the Laffer Curve. There have been instances where money, people and resources have left a state that has imposed higher tax rates on income, resulting in adverse effects of lower tax revenues.

- Being in the top percent of income earners is not as high as one would think. A household, meaning multiple earners, would only have to make $160,000 to be considered in the top ten percent and nearly $200,000 to be considered in the top five percent.

- Lowering or increasing tax rates should be met with spending cuts in government. A tax raise does not justify more spending with a nation that is getting more and more into crippling debt.

- Social Security is a failing program that used to have 159 workers for every 1 retiree. It has shrunk to 2.8 workers to every 1 retiree. The average check issued to recipients is $1,404—barely above the poverty line of $16,240 annually.

- Capitalism has made our lives better through one element: incentives. Capitalism fosters innovation and has helped crippled countries that gained independence from the Soviet Union not only survive but thrive. Our quality of life, even for those in poverty, is significantly better than those of other countries due to our abundance of food, technology, and competition, which has driven down the price for everyday items.

- While health care and food are both necessities, neither is a right. However, food is readily accessible to everyone because competition and innovation make it so. If we treat health care as a commodity, like food, price can be driven down through competition and health care will be more accessible.

DUMB EDUCATION

- Public schools are heavily influenced by teacher unions that have an affiliation to a single party. Teachers are less measured on performance of students and more so on their ability to have successful collective bargaining agreements that benefit them.

- Professors at universities are heavily one-sided to political identities. Democratic professors outnumber Republican professors by an 11.5 to 1 ratio.

- Universities have created strife between those that are diverse in thought from the mainstream narrative pushed on university campuses. This has led to violent protests on campuses from invited speakers that were pro-conservative.

- Safe spaces have become hate spaces that use exclusion to push an unchallenged single narrative used to help "provide for a divide" and set up tribal attitudes.

- Professors are using their platforms to promote radical dogmas with no consequences. Courses have become more of an indoctrination assembly line than an educational free forum.

DUMB CULTURE

- Hollywood is a heavy supporter and donor to the Democratic Party and is quick to oust anyone who does not fall into their group think and, at times, their hypocritical mentality.

- Media conglomerates have helped define and shape our culture. They decide who, what, and how an issue is important for us. Corporations such as Comcast and Warner Media control large fragments of everyday, consumed media that uses this outlet to push their class-dominant agenda.

- Americans do not trust the media anymore. Ninety-two percent of Republicans think the media reports news it knows to be false or purposely misleading. Fifty-three percent of Democrats and seventy-nine percent of Independents also believe this is true.

- Big business is more influential in culture than ever with the rise of the tech industry and social media. These companies have been caught actively suppressing and censoring conservative materials. Social media companies are the biggest violators of free speech and infringe on individual rights to express particular political views.

If we look to the consequences of first, second and third parties from each political action, re-action and non-action, we can avoid dumb politics. There are fringe nut jobs on both the far left and far right that dip equally into the pool of dumb politics. The goal is to recognize dumb politics and avoid becoming part of the blissfully ignorant group that embraces it.

Appendix A

National Socialist German Workers' Party

Written by Adolf Hitler and Anton Drexler, this program was meant to act as a sort of "creed" to the Nazi Party when it was founded in 1920.

1. We demand the union of all Germans in a Great Germany on the basis of the principle of self-determination of all peoples.

2. We demand that the German people have rights equal to those of other nations; and that the Peace Treaties of Versailles and St. Germain shall be abrogated.

3. We demand land and territory (colonies) for the maintenance of our people and the settlement of our surplus population.

4. Only those who are our fellow countrymen can become citizens. Only those who have German blood, regardless of creed, can be our countrymen. Hence no Jew can be a countryman.

5. Those who are not citizens must live in Germany as foreigners and must be subject to the law of aliens.

6. The right to choose the government and determine the laws of the State shall belong only to citizens. We therefore

demand that no public office, of whatever nature, whether in the central government, the province. or the municipality, shall be held by anyone who is not a citizen.

7. We wage war against the corrupt parliamentary administration whereby men are appointed to posts by favor of the party without regard to character and fitness.

8. We demand that the State shall above all undertake to ensure that every citizen shall have the possibility of living decently and earning a livelihood. If it should not be possible to feed the whole population, then aliens (non-citizens) must be expelled from the Reich.

9. Any further immigration of non-Germans must be prevented. We demand that all non-Germans who have entered Germany since August 2, 1914, shall be compelled to leave the Reich immediately.

10. All citizens must possess equal rights and duties.

11. The first duty of every citizen must be to work mentally or physically. No individual shall do any work that offends against the interest of the community to the benefit of all.

Therefore we demand:

12. That all unearned income, and all income that does not arise from work, be abolished.

Breaking the Bondage of Interest

13. Since every war imposes on the people fearful sacrifices in blood and treasure, all personal profit arising from the war must be regarded as treason to the people We therefore demand the total confiscation of all war profits.

14. We demand the nationalization of all trusts.

15. We demand profit-sharing in large industries.

16. We demand a generous increase in old-age pensions.

17. We demand the creation and maintenance of a sound middle-class, the immediate communalization of large stores which will be rented cheaply to small tradespeople, and the strongest consideration must be given to ensure that small traders shall deliver the supplies needed by the State, the provinces and municipalities.

18. We demand an agrarian reform in accordance with our national requirements, and the enactment of a law to expropriate the owners without compensation of any land needed for the common purpose. The abolition of ground rents, and the prohibition of all speculation in land.

19. We demand that ruthless war be waged against those who work to the injury of the common welfare. Traitors, usurers, profiteers, etc., are to be punished with death, regardless of creed or race.

20. We demand that Roman law, which serves a materialist ordering of the world, be replaced by German common law.

21. In order to make it possible for every capable and industrious German to obtain higher education, and thus the opportunity to reach into positions of leadership, the State must assume the responsibility of organizing thoroughly the entire cultural system of the people. The curricula of all educational establishments shall be adapted to practical life. The conception of the State Idea (science of citizenship) must be taught in the schools from the very beginning. We demand that specially talented children of poor parents, whatever their station or occupation, be educated at the expense of the State.

22. The State has the duty to help raise the standard of national health by providing maternity welfare centers, by prohibiting juvenile labor, by increasing physical fitness through the introduction of compulsory games and gymnastics, and by the greatest possible encouragement of associations concerned with the physical education of the young.

23. We demand the abolition of the regular army and the creation of a national (folk) army.

24. We demand that there be a legal campaign against those who propagate deliberate political lies and disseminate them through the press. In order to make possible the creation of a German press, we demand:

    (a) All editors and their assistants on newspapers published in the German language shall be German citizens.

    (b) Non-German newspapers shall only be published with the express permission of the State. They must not be published in the German language.

    (c) All financial interests in or in any way affecting German newspapers shall be forbidden to non-Germans by law, and we demand that the punishment for transgressing this law be the immediate suppression of the newspaper and the expulsion of the non-Germans from the Reich.

Newspapers transgressing against the common welfare shall be suppressed. We demand legal action against those tendencies in art and literature that have a disruptive influence upon the life of our folk, and that any organizations that offend against the foregoing demands shall be dissolved.

25. We demand freedom for all religious faiths in the state, insofar as they do not endanger its existence or offend the moral and ethical sense of the Germanic race.

The party as such represents the point of view of a positive Christianity without binding itself to any one particular confession. It fights against the Jewish materialist spirit within and without, and is convinced that a lasting recovery of our folk can only come about from within on the principle:

COMMON GOOD BEFORE INDIVIDUAL GOOD

26. In order to carry out this program we demand: the creation of a strong central authority in the State, the unconditional authority by the political central parliament of the whole State and all its organizations; the formation of professional committees and of committees representing the several estates of the realm, to ensure that the laws promulgated by the central authority shall be carried out by the federal states; and the leaders of the party undertake to promote the execution of the foregoing points at all costs, if necessary at the sacrifice of their own lives.1

---

1. Source: "The Avalon Project: Program of the National Socialist German Workers' Party," Avalon Project - Documents in Law, History and Diplomacy, accessed August 08, 2018, http://avalon.law.yale.edu/imt/nsdappro.asp.

Notes

Chapter 1—Dumb Politics

1. Feminism. "Women's March Expresses Angst Over Sex-Trafficking Site Shutdown." The Federalist. April 18, 2018. Accessed May 25, 2018. http://thefederalist.com/2018/04/13/womens-march-expresses-angst-sex-trafficking-site-shutdown/.

2. Darby, Luke. "Jimmy Kimmel Says the NRA Has Republicans' Balls in a Money Clip." GQ, 3 Oct. 2017, www.gq.com/story/kimmel-las-vegas-shooting.

3. Democrats." USA Today, Gannett Satellite Information Network, 26 Feb. 2018, www.usatoday.com/story/opinion/2018/02/26/if-nra-owns-republicans-planned-parenthood-owns-democrats-christian-schneider-column/372679002/.

4. Fry, Richard. "For First Time in Modern Era, Living with Parents Edges out Other Living Arrangements for 18- to 34-Year-Olds." Pew Research Center's Social & Demographic Trends Project, 24 May 2016, www.pewsocialtrends.org/2016/05/24/for-first-time-in-modern-era-living-with-parents-edges-out-other-living-arrangements-for-18-to-34-year-olds/.

5. Steinberg, Laurence. "Why We Should Lower the Voting Age to 16." The New York Times, 2 Mar. 2018, www.nytimes.com/2018/03/02/opinion/sunday/voting-age-school-shootings.html.

6. Vargas, Richard Edmond. "Guns Alone Don't Kill People, Patriarchy Kills People." CNN, 1 May 2018, www.cnn.com/2018/05/01/opinions/patriarchy-kills-people-opinion-vargas/index.html.

7. Carapezza, Kirk. "DOJ Looks Into Whether Harvard Discriminates Against Asian-Americans." NPR. August 03, 2017. Accessed May 25, 2018. https://www.npr.org/2017/08/03/541430130/trump-admin-looking-into-whether-harvard-discriminates-against-asian-americans.

8. Hill, Libby. "Pepsi Apologizes, Pulls Controversial Kendall Jenner Ad." Los Angeles Times, 5 Apr. 2017, www.latimes.com/entertainment/la-et-entertainment-news-updates-april-never-mind-pepsi-s-sorry-about-that-1491416502-htmlstory.html.

9. King, Alexandra. "Rachel Dolezal: 'Race Is a Social Construct.'" CNN, 1 Apr. 2017, www.cnn.com/2017/04/01/us/rachel-dolezal-race-social-construct-cnntv/index.html.

10. "Census Finds Least Diverse Part of Nation." ABC News, abcnews.go.com/US/story?id=93608&page=1.

11. "Letter to Thomas Auld (September 3, 1848)." Plessy v. Ferguson | The Gilder Lehrman Center for the Study of Slavery, Resistance, and Abolition. Accessed September 01, 2018. https://glc.yale.edu/letter-thomas-auld-september-3-1848.

12. McKay, Hollie. "Critics Slam MSNBC Host's Claim That Kids Belong to Community, Not Parents." Fox News. Accessed September 01, 2018. http://www.foxnews.com/entertainment/2013/04/09/critics-slam-msnbc-hosts-claim-that-kids-belong-to-community-not-parents.html.

13. Dionne Jr., Special to the New York Times, E.J. "Biden Joins Campaign for the Presidency." The New York Times. June 10, 1987. Accessed September 01, 2018. https://www.nytimes.com/1987/06/10/us/biden-joins-campaign-for-the-presidency.html.

CHAPTER 2—DUMB NAME CALLING

1. Reilly, Katie. "Hillary Clinton Transcript: 'Basket of Deplorables' Comment." Time. September 10, 2016.

Accessed August 08, 2018. http://time.com/4486502/
hillary-clinton-basket-of-deplorables-transcript/.

2. Albright, Madeleine. "Will We Stop Trump Before It's Too Late?"
   The New York Times. April 06, 2018. Accessed August 08, 2018.
   https://www.nytimes.com/2018/04/06/opinion/sunday/trump-fascism-
   madeleine-albright.html.

3. Dickens, Geoffrey. "Flashback: MSNBC Hosts Called Bush
   Fascist, Murderous and War Criminal, Never Faced Suspensions."
   NewsBusters. June 30, 2011. Accessed August 08, 2018. https://
   www.newsbusters.org/blogs/nb/geoffrey-dickens/2011/06/30/
   flashback-msnbc-hosts-called-bush-fascist-murderous-and-war.

4. Stoll, Ira. "Fears of Trump as Fascist Echo Similar Warnings
   Against Ronald Reagan." The New York Sun. February 29, 2016.
   Accessed August 08, 2018. https://www.nysun.com/national/
   fears-of-trump-as-fascist-echo-similar-warnings/89476/.

5. Grossu, Arina. "Margaret Sanger, Racist Eugenicist Extraordinaire."
   The Washington Times. May 05, 2014. Accessed August 08,
   2018. https://www.washingtontimes.com/news/2014/may/5/
   grossu-margaret-sanger-eugenicist/.

6. Boaz, David. "Hitler, Mussolini, Roosevelt." Cato Institute. September
   28, 2007. Accessed August 08, 2018. https://www.cato.org/publications/
   commentary/hitler-mussolini-roosevelt.

7. Zauzmer, Julie. "Holocaust Study: Two-thirds of Millennials Don't
   Know What Auschwitz Is." The Washington Post. April 12, 2018.
   Accessed August 08, 2018. https://www.washingtonpost.com/news/
   acts-of-faith/wp/2018/04/12/two-thirds-of-millennials-dont-know-what-
   auschwitz-is-according-to-study-of-fading-holocaust-knowledge/?utm_
   term=.685d5ecc1054.

8. "Racism." Merriam-Webster. Accessed August 08, 2018. https://www.
   merriam-webster.com/dictionary/racism.

9. "Who Causes More Car Accidents? The Data May Surprise You »
   Traffic Safety Resource Center." Traffic Safety Resource Center. August
   11, 2017. Accessed August 08, 2018. https://www.trafficsafetystore.
   com/blog/who-causes-accidents/.

CHAPTER 3—DUMB IMMIGRATION

1. Moons, Michelle. "WATCH: 'Professor Occupy' Lisa Fithian Directs Open Borders DC Protest." Breitbart. July 01, 2018. Accessed August 07, 2018. https://www.breitbart.com/big-government/2018/07/01/watch-professor-occupy-lisa-fithian-directs-open-borders-dc-protest/.

2. Payton, Matt. "Quanell X Comes up with Perfect Argument to Shut down Fox News Host's Rant." The Independent. September 30, 2016. Accessed August 07, 2018. https://www.independent.co.uk/news/world/americas/black-activist-quanell-x-tells-radio-host-fox-news-white-people-stole-the-us-and-should-all-go-home-a7337511.html.

3. Hagan, Shelly. "Where U.S. Unemployment Is Still Sky-High: Indian Reservations." Bloomberg.com. April 05, 2018. Accessed August 07, 2018. https://www.bloomberg.com/news/articles/2018-04-05/where-u-s-unemployment-is-still-sky-high-indian-reservations.

4. Riley, Naomi Schaefer. "Here's One Way to Help Native Americans: Property Rights." The Atlantic. August 01, 2016. Accessed August 07, 2018. https://www.theatlantic.com/politics/archive/2016/07/native-americans-property-rights/492941/.

5. Regan, Shawn E., and Terry L. Anderson. "The Energy Wealth of Indian Nations." LSU Law Digital Commons. Accessed August 08, 2018. https://digitalcommons.law.lsu.edu/jelr/vol3/iss1/9/.

6. Marshall, Serena. "Obama Has Deported More People Than Any Other President." ABC News. August 29, 2016. Accessed August 08, 2018. https://abcnews.go.com/Politics/obamas-deportation-policy-numbers/story?id=41715661.

7. Koshar, Rudy. "Fascism Depends on Walls." The Huffington Post. June 25, 2017. Accessed August 08, 2018. http://www.huffingtonpost.com/rudy-koshar/fascism-depends-on-walls_b_10638688.html.

8. Walsh, Sean Collins. "Congressman Beto O'Rourke: Trump's Wall Is 'racist'." Statesman. January 27, 2017. Accessed August 08, 2018. http://www.statesman.com/news/national-govt--politics/congressman-beto-rourke-trump-wall-racist/SRCdQUqslym7z53k6m54oJ/.

9. Bob.Price.Texas. "50 Pounds of Cartel Meth Busted in 'Safe Border City' El Paso." Breitbart. April 13, 2016. Accessed August 08, 2018. http://www.breitbart.com/texas/2016/04/12/50-pounds-cartel-meth-busted-safe-city-el-paso/.

10. Martinez, Aaron. "Woman, 75, Arrested, Accused of Trying to Smuggle Heroin in Purse, SUV in Tornillo." El Paso Times. May 22, 2018. Accessed August 08, 2018. https://www.elpasotimes.com/story/news/crime/2018/05/22/woman-75-arrested-suspicion-smuggling-heroin-purse-vehicle/634433002/.

11. Parks, Maryalice. "Bernie Sanders on the Border: 'We Don't Need a Wall'." ABC News. March 19, 2016. Accessed August 08, 2018. http://abcnews.go.com/Politics/bernie-sanders-border-dont-wall/story?id=37779082.

12. "Census Finds Least Diverse Part of Nation." ABC News. Accessed August 08, 2018. http://abcnews.go.com/US/story?id=93608&page=1.

13. "Shea-Porter Statement on President Trump's State of the Union Address." Congresswoman Carol Shea-Porter. January 31, 2018. Accessed August 08, 2018. https://shea-porter.house.gov/media/press-releases/shea-porter-statement-president-trump-s-state-union-address.

14. Bob.Price.Texas. "Mexico's Government Warns U.S.A. to Not Build Border Walls." Breitbart. April 30, 2017. Accessed August 08, 2018. http://www.breitbart.com/texas/2017/04/28/mexicos-government-warns-u-s-not-build-border-walls/.

15. "Trump's Border Wall Finds Its Weirdest Critic Yet." The Daily Caller. Accessed August 08, 2018. http://dailycaller.com/2017/03/23/trumps-border-wall-finds-its-weirdest-critic-yet/.

16. Associated Press. "Mexico Is More Dangerous than Ever." New York Post. January 22, 2018. Accessed August 08, 2018. https://nypost.com/2018/01/22/mexico-is-more-dangerous-than-ever/.

17. Ortiz, Ildefonso. "News Outlets Use Fake Twitter Accounts to Cash in on 'El Chapo'." Breitbart. January 11, 2016. Accessed August 08, 2018. http://www.breitbart.com/texas/2016/01/10/news-outlets-continue-using-debunked-twitter-accounts-to-glorify-murderous-narcos/.

18. "Durango Becoming Ground Zero for Zetas-Sinaloa Cartel Battle." InSight Crime. October 06, 2017. Accessed August 08, 2018. https://www.insightcrime.org/news/analysis/durango-ground-zero-for-zetas-sinaloa-cartel-battle/.

19. Garza, Antonio. "Mexican Journalists Killed Seeking Truth." Star-telegram. Accessed August 08, 2018. https://www.star-telegram.com/opinion/opn-columns-blogs/other-voices/article154131684.html.

20. Suarez, Ray, and Carrie Kahn. "Mexican Crime Reporter Gumaro Pérez Aguilando Shot To Death." NPR. December 20, 2017. Accessed August 08, 2018. https://www.npr.org/2017/12/20/572376155/mexican-crime-reporter-gumaro-perez-aguilando-shot-to-death.

21. "Miroslava Breach Third Mexican Journalist to Be Killed This Month." BBC News. March 23, 2017. Accessed August 08, 2018. https://www.bbc.com/news/world-latin-america-39376061.

22. Linthicum, Kate. "Another Journalist Has Been Killed in Mexico - the Sixth This Year." Los Angeles Times. May 29, 2018. Accessed August 08, 2018. http://www.latimes.com/world/mexico-americas/la-fg-mexico-journalist-killed-20180529-story.html.

23. Chronicles, Cartel. "GRAPHIC: Los Zetas Cartel Kill U.S. Woman and 2 Daughters in Weekend Massacre That Left 19 Dead." Breitbart. July 11, 2016. Accessed August 08, 2018. https://www.breitbart.com/texas/2016/07/11/graphic-los-zetas-cartel-kill-u-s-woman-2-daughters-weekend-massacre-left-19-dead/.

24. Staff, Independent. "Cartel Leader Who Dismembered Six-year-old Girl While She Was Still Alive Jailed for Life." The Independent. June 30, 2017. Accessed August 08, 2018. https://www.independent.co.uk/news/world/americas/marciano-millan-vasquez-jailed-life-mexican-cartel-leader-dismembered-six-year-old-girl-a7816511.html.

25. "Opinion: Mexican Drug Cartels Are Worse than ISIL." Al Jazeera America. Accessed August 08, 2018. http://america.aljazeera.com/opinions/2014/10/isil-vs-mexican-drugcartelsunitedstatesislamophobia.html.

26. "Three Undocumented Immigrants Arrested in Kidnapping of Orange County Attorney." KBMT. May 16, 2017. Accessed August

08, 2018. https://www.12newsnow.com/article/news/local/three-undocumented-immigrants-arrested-in-kidnapping-of-orange-county-attorney/439794443.

27. "Suspect in US Illegally before Shooting Death of Mesa Store Clerk." Phoenix News - Arizona's Family. January 22, 2015. Accessed August 08, 2018. http://www.azfamily.com/story/27911249/suspect-caught-in-deadly-mesa-store-shooting.

28. Christian, Carol. "21-year-old Immigrant Convicted in Beating Death of Former Pearland Classmate." Houston Chronicle. January 29, 2013. Accessed August 08, 2018. http://www.chron.com/news/houston-texas/houston/article/21-year-old-convicted-in-beating-death-of-former-4233272.php.

29. "Mexican Cartel Allegedly Hired MS-13 To Carry Out Torture Operation In Minnesota." Fox News. Accessed August 08, 2018. http://www.foxnews.com/world/2014/05/06/mexican-cartel-allegedly-hired-ms-13-to-carry-out-torture-operation-in.html.

30. "Opioid Overdose." Centers for Disease Control and Prevention. January 26, 2017. Accessed August 08, 2018. https://www.cdc.gov/drugoverdose/data/heroin.html.

31. United States. Drug Enforcement Administration. 2015 National Prescription Drug Threat Assessment Summary. United States: ICGtesting.com, 2015.

32. "U.S. Border Patrol Fiscal Year 2017 Sector Profile." Border Patrol Overview | U.S. Customs and Border Protection. Accessed August 08, 2018. https://www.cbp.gov/document/stats/us-border-patrol-fiscal-year-2017-sector-profile.

33. National Institute on Drug Abuse. "What Is the Scope of Heroin Use in the United States?" NIDA. Accessed August 08, 2018. https://www.drugabuse.gov/publications/research-reports/heroin/scope-heroin-use-in-united-states.

34. "Opioid Overdose." Centers for Disease Control and Prevention. August 30, 2017. Accessed August 08, 2018. https://www.cdc.gov/drugoverdose/epidemic/.

35. "Groups Want Trump to Close Loophole Allowing Illegal Immigrants to Abuse Tax Credits." Fox News. Accessed August 08, 2018. http://www.foxnews.com/politics/2017/02/09/groups-want-trump-to-close-loophole-allowing-illegal-immigrants-to-abuse-tax-credits.html.

36. O'Brien, Matt, and Spencer Raley. "The Cost of Illegal Immigration to US Taxpayers | FAIR." Federation for American Immigration Reform. September 27, 2017. Accessed August 08, 2018. https://fairus.org/issue/publications-resources/fiscal-burden-illegal-immigration-united-states-taxpayers.

37. Two Main Forces Drove the Trend: Mexico's Weak Currency. "Mexicans in U.S. Send Cash Home in Record Numbers." CNNMoney. Accessed August 08, 2018. http://money.cnn.com/2018/01/02/news/economy/mexico-remittances/index.html.

38. Borjas, George J., Michael Grunwald, Beth Macy, Edward McClelland, and Jack Shafer. "Yes, Immigration Hurts American Workers." About Us. Accessed August 08, 2018. https://www.politico.com/magazine/story/2016/09/trump-clinton-immigration-economy-unemployment-jobs-214216.

39. "Immigration and the American Worker." CIS.org. Accessed August 08, 2018. https://cis.org/Report/Immigration-and-American-Worker.

40. "Mexico: Migration Authorities Unlawfully Turning Back Thousands of Central Americans to Possible Death." January 23, 2018. Accessed September 13, 2018. https://www.amnesty.org/en/latest/news/2018/01/mexico-migration-authorities-unlawfully-turning-back-thousands-of-central-americans-to-possible-death/.

41. Connor, Phillip, and Gustavo López. "5 Facts about the U.S. Rank in Worldwide Migration." Pew Research Center. May 18, 2016. Accessed August 08, 2018. http://www.pewresearch.org/fact-tank/2016/05/18/5-facts-about-the-u-s-rank-in-worldwide-migration/.

42. "Harvard-Harris Poll: 76% of Registered Voters Do Not Support 'Open Borders'." CNS News. July 05, 2018. Accessed August 08, 2018. https://www.cnsnews.com/news/article/jonathan-mizrahi/harvard-harris-poll-76-registered-voters-do-not-support-open-borders.

CHAPTER 4—DUMB ECONOMICS

1. Rasmussen Poll. "46% Favor Government Guaranteed Jobs for All." Rasmussen Reports. Accessed August 08, 2018. http://www.rasmussenreports.com/public_content/politics/general_politics/april_2018/46_favor_government_guaranteed_jobs_for_all.

2. Hazlitt, Henry. *Economics in One Lesson*. New York, NY: Three Rivers Press, 1979, p. 17

3. Hough, Austin. "Sen. McCaskill right about small business job creation." Politifact Missouri, March 17, 2017. https://www.politifact.com/missouri/statements/2017/mar/17/claire-mccaskill/sen-mccaskill-right-about-small-business-job-creat/

4. Luca, Dara Lee, and Michael Luca. "Survival of the Fittest: The Impact of the Minimum Wage on Firm Exit." *SSRN Electronic Journal*, 2017. doi:10.2139/ssrn.2951110.

5. Salem, Houman. "Leaving for Las Vegas: California's Minimum Wage Law Leaves Businesses No Choice." LA Times. January 6, 2017. http://www.latimes.com/opinion/op-ed/la-oe-salem-minimum-wage-20170102-story.html.

6. Higgins, Sean, and Ted S. Warren. "Study: Seattle's Minimum Wage Is Hurting the Poor." Washington Examiner. June 26, 2017. Accessed August 08, 2018. https://www.washingtonexaminer.com/study-seattles-minimum-wage-is-hurting-the-poor.

7. Reisman, George. "How Minimum Wage Laws Increase Poverty | George Reisman." Mises Institute. April 02, 2014. Accessed August 08, 2018. https://mises.org/library/how-minimum-wage-laws-increase-poverty.

8. Sanadaji, Nima. "5 Myths About Nordic Socialism Peddled By the Left." The Stream. September 07, 2016. Accessed August 08, 2018. https://stream.org/5-myths-nordic-socialism-mislead-the-american-left/.

9. "What the Left Gets Wrong About Scandinavia." Fortune. Accessed August 08, 2018. http://fortune.com/2016/01/26/democrat-bernie-sanders-scandinavia-socialism/.

10. Sowell, Thomas. Basic Economics A Common Sense Guide to the Economy. Fifth ed. New York, NY: Basic Books, 2015, p.426-428

11. "The Federal Budget in 2017: An Infographic." Congressional Budget Office. Accessed August 08, 2018. https://www.cbo.gov/publication/53624.

12. Jr., Clyde Wayne Crews. "How Many Federal Agencies Exist? We Can't Drain The Swamp Until We Know." Forbes. July 05, 2017. Accessed August 08, 2018. https://www.forbes.com/sites/waynecrews/2017/07/05/how-many-federal-agencies-exist-we-cant-drain-the-swamp-until-we-know/#217903161aa2.

13. "The Federal Budget in 2017: An Infographic." Congressional Budget Office. Accessed August 08, 2018. https://www.cbo.gov/publication/53624.

14. Collinson, Catherine. Millennial Workers: An Emerging Generation of Super Savers. 2014. 15th Annual Transamerica Retirement Survey July 2014, p.10.

15. United States. Congressional Research Service. The Social Security Retirement Age: In Brief. By Gary Sidor, p.1.

16. "Social Security." Social Security History. Accessed August 08, 2018. https://www.ssa.gov/history/ratios.html.

17. Pleat, Zachary. "Dozens of Local Fox Affiliates Run Misleading Segments Pushing Social Security Benefit Cuts." Media Matters for America. May 30, 2018. Accessed August 08, 2018. https://www.mediamatters.org/blog/2018/05/30/dozens-local-fox-affiliates-run-misleading-segments-pushing-social-security-benefit-cuts/220334.

18. DeSilver, Drew. "5 Facts about Social Security." Pew Research Center. August 18, 2015. Accessed August 08, 2018. http://www.pewresearch.org/fact-tank/2015/08/18/5-facts-about-social-security/.

19. Ryan, Paul. "Rep. Paul Ryan 1st District of Wisconsin." FIRST STEP: STOPPING THE RAID ON SOCIAL SECURITY. July 7, 2005 Accessed August 08, 2018. https://paulryan.house.gov/news/documentsingle.aspx?DocumentID=247886.

20. "COUNTRY COMPARISON :: GDP - PER CAPITA (PPP)." Central Intelligence Agency. Accessed August 08, 2018. https://www.cia.gov/library/publications/the-world-factbook/rankorder/2004rank.html.

21. Worstall, Tim. "Astonishing Numbers: America's Poor Still Live Better Than Most Of The Rest Of Humanity." Forbes. June 01, 2013. Accessed August 08, 2018. https://www.forbes.com/sites/timworstall/2013/06/01/astonishing-numbers-americas-poor-still-live-better-than-most-of-the-rest-of-humanity/#2db6541254ef.

22. Rector, Robert. "The War on Poverty: 50 Years of Failure." The Heritage Foundation. September 23, 2014. Accessed August 08, 2018. https://www.heritage.org/marriage-and-family/commentary/the-war-poverty-50-years-failure.

23. Shapiro, Ben. "There's No Such Thing as 'Crony Capitalism'." Townhall. September 07, 2011. Accessed August 08, 2018. https://townhall.com/columnists/benshapiro/2011/09/07/theres-no-such-thing-as-crony-capitalism-n1175043.

24. Veterans' Health Administration. "Veterans' Health Administration." Go to VA.gov. June 10, 2009. Accessed August 08, 2018. https://www.va.gov/health/aboutvha.asp.

CHAPTER 5—DUMB EDUCATION

1. Barry, Ellen. "In Sweden's Preschools, Boys Learn to Dance and Girls Learn to Yell." The New York Times. March 24, 2018. Accessed August 08, 2018. https://www.nytimes.com/2018/03/24/world/europe/sweden-gender-neutral-preschools.html?mtrref=www.nytimes.com&login=email&auth=login-email.

2. Masci, David, Anna Brown, and Jocelyn Kiley. "5 Facts about Same-sex Marriage." Pew Research Center. June 26, 2017. Accessed August 08, 2018. http://www.pewresearch.org/fact-tank/2017/06/26/same-sex-marriage/.

3. Parke, Caleb. "Public School in Minnesota Requires English Course Aimed at Eradicating White Privilege." Fox News. November 02, 2017.

Accessed August 08, 2018. http://www.foxnews.com/us/2017/11/02/public-school-in-minnesota-requires-english-course-aimed-at-eradicating-white-privilege.html.

4. Arguello, Lorenzo. "Utah High School Mascot Won't Be 'Cougars' Because It Would Offend Women." Business Insider. January 19, 2012. Accessed August 08, 2018. https://www.businessinsider.com/utah-high-school-mascot-not-cougars-because-it-would-offend-women-2012-1.

5. Egelko, Bob. "Court Backs Morgan Hill School in Flag Dispute." SFGate. November 30, 2011. Accessed August 08, 2018. https://www.sfgate.com/bayarea/article/Court-backs-Morgan-Hill-school-in-flag-dispute-2323579.php.

6. Jr., Cleve R. Wootson. "'To Be White Is to Be Racist, Period,' a High School Teacher Told His Class." The Washington Post. October 21, 2016. Accessed August 08, 2018. https://www.washingtonpost.com/news/education/wp/2016/10/19/to-be-white-is-to-be-racist-period-a-high-school-teacher-told-his-class/?utm_term=.e9012b193788.

7. Shah, Nirvi. "American Federation of Teachers Endorses Hillary Clinton for President." About Us. July 11, 2015. Accessed August 08, 2018. https://www.politico.com/story/2015/07/aft-endorses-hillary-clinton-for-president-119988.

8. LoVerde, Joe. "Mulgrew: Union Is Going All out for Hillary." How Toxic Is Toxic? | United Federation of Teachers. Accessed August 08, 2018. http://www.uft.org/news-stories/mulgrew-union-going-all-out-hillary.

9. "The Importance of Teachers Supporting Their Unions." ToBecomeaTeacher.org. November 20, 2017. Accessed August 08, 2018. http://tobecomeateacher.org/the-importance-of-teachers-supporting-their-unions/.

10. "By the Numbers: Teachers Union Political Contributions in 2016." Fox News. Accessed August 08, 2018. http://www.foxnews.com/politics/2017/01/17/by-numbers-teachers-union-political-contributions-in-2016.html.

11. DeSilver, Drew. "U.S. Students' Academic Achievement Still Lags That of Their Peers in Many Other Countries." Pew Research Center.

February 15, 2017. Accessed August 08, 2018. http://www.pewresearch. org/fact-tank/2017/02/15/u-s-students-internationally-math-science/.

12. Loewus, Liana. "The Nation's Teaching Force Is Still Mostly White and Female." Education Week. June 20, 2018. Accessed August 08, 2018. https://www.edweek.org/ew/articles/2017/08/15/the-nations-teaching-force-is-still-mostly.html.

13. Langbert, Mitchell, Anthony Quain, and Daniel Klein. "Faculty Voter Registration in Economics, History, Journalism, Law, and Psychology." Econ Journal Watch, September 2016, 422-51.

14. Brown, Spencer. "Commencement Season In The Age Of #MeToo: Conservative Women Still Left Out." Young America's Foundation. May 15, 2018. Accessed August 08, 2018. https://www.yaf.org/news/commencement-season-in-the-age-of-metoo-conservative-women-still-left-out/.

15. "White Students Barred from Funded RSU Student Group Event." Ryersonian.ca. March 25, 2015. Accessed August 08, 2018. http://ryer-sonian.ca/white-students-barred-from-funded-rsu-student-group-event/.

16. Ansari, Aeman. "Ethnic Minorities Deserve Safe Spaces Without White People." HuffPost Canada. May 18, 2015. Accessed August 08, 2018. https://www.huffingtonpost.ca/aeman-ansari/ethnic-safe-spaces_b_6897176.html.

17. Clark, Mason. "UMich Students Demand No-whites-allowed Space to Plot 'social Justice' Activism." The College Fix. February 23, 2017. Accessed August 08, 2018. https://www.thecollegefix.com/post/31322/.

18. Vivanco, Leonor, and Dawn Rhodes. "U. of C. Tells Incoming Freshmen It Does Not Support 'trigger Warnings' or 'safe Spaces'." Chicagotribune.com. August 26, 2016. Accessed August 08, 2018. http://www.chicagotribune.com/news/local/breaking/ct-university-of-chicago-safe-spaces-letter-met-20160825-story.html.

19. "Check Your Privilege." Tuition and Fees Schedule for Academic Year 2017-18 | MyUSF. Accessed August 08, 2018. https://myusf.usfca.edu/student-life/intercultural-center/check-your-privilege.

20. Gockowski, Anthony. "Prof Calls Whites 'inhuman Assholes,' Says 'let Them Die'." Campus Reform. June 20, 2017. Accessed August 08, 2018. https://www.campusreform.org/?ID=9334.

21. "Let Them Fucking Die–Son of Baldwin–Medium." Medium. June 16, 2017. Accessed August 08, 2018. https://medium.com/@ SonofBaldwin/let-them-fucking-die-c316eee34212.

22. Gray, Melissa. "Drexel Professor Resigns amid Threats over Controversial Tweets." CNN. December 29, 2017. Accessed August 08, 2018. https://www.cnn.com/2017/12/28/us/drexel-university-professor-resigns/index.html.

23. Fredericks, Bob. "This College Professor Is Happy 'racist' Barbara Bush Is Dead." New York Post. April 18, 2018. Accessed August 08, 2018. https://nypost.com/2018/04/18/this-college-professor-is-happy-racist-barbara-bush-is-dead/.

24. Appleton, Aleksandra. "This Is What Randa Jarrar Has to Say about Her Barbara Bush Tweets." Fresnobee. April 24, 2018. Accessed August 08, 2018. https://www.fresnobee.com/news/local/education/article209702619.html.

CHAPTER 6—DUMB CULTURE

1. McCarthy, Andrew C. "Bill Ayers: Unrepentant LYING Terrorist." National Review. April 08, 2015. Accessed August 08, 2018. https://www.nationalreview.com/corner/bill-ayers-unrepentant-lying-terrorist-andrew-c-mccarthy/.

2. "JOANNE DEBORAH CHESIMARD." FBI. April 12, 2013. Accessed August 08, 2018. https://www.fbi.gov/wanted/wanted_terrorists/joanne-deborah-chesimard.

3. CBS News. "Who Is Saul Alinsky?" CBS News. July 20, 2016. Accessed August 08, 2018. https://www.cbsnews.com/news/who-is-saul-alinsky/.

4. Bond, Paul. "James Woods: 'I Don't Expect to Work Again' in Hollywood." The Hollywood Reporter. October 10, 2013. Accessed

August 08, 2018. https://www.hollywoodreporter.com/news/
james-woods-i-dont-expect-646351.

5. Jaafar, Ali. "Idris Elba Posts Full Text Of Powerful Diversity Speech
    Online." Deadline. January 20, 2016. Accessed August 08, 2018. https://
    deadline.com/2016/01/idris-elba-posts-full-text-of-powerful-diversity-
    speech-online-1201686614/.

6. "Jeffrey Katzenberg Net Worth." Celebrity Net Worth. October 03,
    2016. Accessed August 08, 2018. https://www.celebritynetworth.com/
    richest-businessmen/producers/jeffrey-katzenberg-net-worth/.

7. Gross, Neil. "Why Is Hollywood So Liberal?" The New York
    Times. January 27, 2018. Accessed August 08, 2018. https://www.
    nytimes.com/2018/01/27/opinion/sunday/hollywood-liberal.html.

8. Delbyck, Cole. "Madonna Opens Amy Schumer's Show Offering
    Blow Jobs To Hillary Voters." The Huffington Post. October 25, 2016.
    Accessed August 08, 2018. https://www.huffingtonpost.com/entry/
    madonna-opens-amy-schumers-stand-up-show-by-offering-to-blow-
    hillary-voters_us_5807aa3de4b0dd54ce36f354.

9. Richardson, Valerie. "Samuel L. Jackson Says He
    Isn't Moving to South Africa despite Trump Victory." The
    Washington Times. November 18, 2016. Accessed August 08,
    2018. https://www.washingtontimes.com/news/2016/nov/18/
    samuel-l-jackson-says-he-isnt-moving-south-africa-/.

10. Lewis, Hilary. "Chelsea Handler Insists She'll Leave
    the U.S. If Donald Trump Becomes President." The
    Hollywood Reporter. May 29, 2018. Accessed August
    08, 2018. https://www.hollywoodreporter.com/news/
    chelsea-handler-will-leave-us-donald-trump-becomes-president-892929.

11. Baluja, Tamara. "Lena Dunham Vows to Move to Vancouver
    If Trump Becomes President | CBC News." CBCnews. April 27,
    2016. Accessed August 08, 2018. http://www.cbc.ca/news/canada/
    british-columbia/lena-dunham-vancouver-trump-1.3554533.

12. Kassam, Ashifa, and Benjamin Lee. "'I Really Will': The Stars Who
    Didn't Move to Canada When Trump Won." The Guardian. January

22, 2018. Accessed August 08, 2018. https://www.theguardian.com/world/2018/jan/22/move-to-canada-celebrities-donald-trump.

13. Key, Pam. "Whoopi Threatens to Leave U.S. Over Trump: 'You Can't Blame Immigrants' for Country's Problems." Breitbart. January 20, 2016. Accessed August 08, 2018. https://www.breitbart.com/video/2016/01/20/whoopi-threatens-to-leave-u-s-over-trump-you-cant-blame-immigrants-for-countrys-problems/.

14. Duboff, Josh. "Miley Cyrus Says She'll Leave the Country If Donald Trump Becomes President." The Hive. March 03, 2016. Accessed August 08, 2018. https://www.vanityfair.com/hollywood/2016/03/miley-cyrus-donald-trump-instagrams.

15. Bacardi, Francesca. "Amy Schumer: I'll Move to Spain If Donald Trump Is Elected President." E! Online. September 07, 2016. Accessed August 08, 2018. https://www.eonline.com/news/792771/amy-schumer-is-going-to-move-to-spain-if-donald-trump-is-elected-president.

16. "Is Stephen Baldwin the First Actor to Threaten to Leave the Country If Obama Wins?" New York Magazine. Accessed August 08, 2018. http://nymag.com/daily/intelligencer/2008/07/is_stephen_baldwin_the_first_a.html.

17. "Climate." Conservation International. Accessed August 08, 2018. https://www.conservation.org/what/Pages/Climate.aspx.

18. Nolte, John. "Elitist Enviro-Hypocrisy: Harrison Ford's Cheeseburger Runs." Breitbart. February 26, 2010. Accessed August 08, 2018. https://www.breitbart.com/big-hollywood/2010/02/26/elitist-enviro-hypocrisy-harrison-fords-cheeseburger-runs/.

19. Bitette, Nicole. "Tina Fey Blasts White Women Who Voted for Trump for Wanting to 'go Back to Watching HGTV' - NY Daily News." Nydailynews.com. April 01, 2017. Accessed August 08, 2018. http://www.nydailynews.com/entertainment/tina-fey-blasts-white-women-voted-trump-article-1.3016039.

20. "Caught On A Hot Mic In 1992, Larry King Assures Bill Clinton: "Ted Turner Would Serve You"." Zero Hedge. August 26, 2016. Accessed August 08, 2018. https://www.zerohedge.com/news/2016-08-26/caught-

hot-mic-1992-larry-king-assures-bill-clinton-ted-turner-would-serve-you.

21. Winkelmeyer/Getty Images for The Rush Philan, Matt. "HLN Cancels Dr. Drew's Show Days After He Repeated Trump Talking Points on Hillary's Health." Vulture. August 26, 2016. Accessed August 08, 2018. http://www.vulture.com/2016/08/dr-drew-canceled-after-hillary-health-remarks.html.

22. "Ted Turner Endorses Hillary Clinton for President." Timesfreepress.com. October 26, 2016. Accessed August 08, 2018. https://www.timesfreepress.com/news/politics/elections/story/2016/oct/10/ted-turner-endorses-hillary-clinton-president/391243/.

23. Baranauckas, Carla. "Samantha Bee Slams 'Feckless C**t' Ivanka Trump For Not Doing Something About Immigration." The Huffington Post. May 31, 2018. Accessed August 08, 2018. https://www.huffingtonpost.com/entry/samantha-bee-calls-out-ivanka-trump_us_5b0f8d95e4b0fcd6a833715d.

24. Adams, Becket. "Zucker: Fair to Say CNN Was 'a Little Too Liberal'." Washington Examiner. May 02, 2016. Accessed August 08, 2018. https://www.washingtonexaminer.com/zucker-fair-to-say-cnn-was-a-little-too-liberal.

25. Jacobson, Louis. "Meme Says Hillary Clinton's Top Donors Are Banks and Corporations, Bernie Sanders' Are Labor Unions." Politifact. July 7, 2015. Accessed August 08, 2018. https://www.politifact.com/truth-o-meter/statements/2015/jul/07/facebook-posts/meme-says-hillary-clintons-top-donors-are-banks-an/.

26. Continetti, Matthew. "How Comcast Bought the Democratic Party." National Review. April 07, 2014. Accessed August 08, 2018. https://www.nationalreview.com/2014/04/how-comcast-bought-democratic-party-matthew-continetti/.

27. Langlois, Shawn. "How Biased Is Your News Source? You Probably Won't Agree with This Chart." MarketWatch. April 21, 2018. Accessed August 08, 2018. https://www.marketwatch.com/story/how-biased-is-your-news-source-you-probably-wont-agree-with-this-chart-2018-02-28.

28. Harper, Jennifer. "Fox News Channel Rated No. 1 in Cable News for past 16 Years, Says Nielsen Media Research." The Washington Times. April 03, 2018. Accessed August 08, 2018. https://www.washingtontimes.com/news/2018/apr/3/fox-news-channel-rated-no-1-in-cable-news-for-past/.

29. Fischer, Sara. "92% of Republicans Think Media Intentionally Reports Fake News." Axios. June 27, 1970. Accessed August 08, 2018. https://www.axios.com/trump-effect-92-percent-republicans-media-fake-news-9c1bbf70-0054-41dd-b506-0869bb10f08c.html.

30. Cillizza, Chris. "Millennials Don't Trust Anyone. That's a Big Deal." The Washington Post. April 30, 2015. Accessed August 08, 2018. https://www.washingtonpost.com/news/the-fix/wp/2015/04/30/millennials-dont-trust-anyone-what-else-is-new/?utm_term=.5c70de2c7627.

31. Dulis, Ezra. "Wikileaks: Journalists Dined at Top Clinton Staffers' Homes Days Before Hillary's Campaign Launch." Breitbart. October 18, 2016. Accessed August 08, 2018. https://www.breitbart.com/big-journalism/2016/10/17/wikileaks-journalists-clinton-staff-homes-before-hillarys-campaign-launch/.

32. "Hillary Clinton's 10 Biggest Corporate Donors In The S&P 500." Forbes. Accessed August 08, 2018. https://www.forbes.com/pictures/emdk45ehhgg/hillary-clintons-10-big/#7bfc83463629.

33. "Apple Inc: Recipients." OpenSecrets. Accessed August 08, 2018. https://www.opensecrets.org/orgs/toprecips.php?id=D000021754&type=P&sort=A&cycle=2016.

34. Nunez, Michael. "Former Facebook Workers: We Routinely Suppressed Conservative News." Gizmodo. May 10, 2016. Accessed August 08, 2018. https://gizmodo.com/former-facebook-workers-we-routinely-suppressed conser 1775461006.

35. Saavedra, Ryan. "BOMBSHELL REPORT: Twitter Employees Admit To Censoring Conservatives, Banning Them For Political Reasons." Daily Wire. January 11, 2018. Accessed August 08, 2018. https://www.dailywire.com/news/25744/bombshell-report-twitter-admits-censoring-ryan-saavedra.

36. Smith, Aaron, and Monica Anderson. "Social Media Use in 2018." Pew Research Center: Internet, Science & Tech. March 01, 2018. Accessed August 08, 2018. http://www.pewinternet.org/2018/03/01/social-media-use-in-2018/.

37. Shearer, Elisa, and Jeffrey Gottfried. "News Use Across Social Media Platforms 2017." Pew Research Center's Journalism Project. September 07, 2017. Accessed August 08, 2018. http://www.journalism.org/2017/09/07/news-use-across-social-media-platforms-2017/.

38. Fernholz, Tim. "Leaked Emails Show Eric Schmidt Played a Crucial Role in Team Hillary's Election Tech." Quartz. November 01, 2016. Accessed August 08, 2018. https://qz.com/823922/eric-schmidt-played-a-crucial-role-in-team-hillarys-election-tech/.

39. Romm, Tony. "Reid Hoffman Could Spend Hundreds of Millions to Fix Some of the Country's Biggest Political Problems." Recode. May 31, 2017. Accessed August 08, 2018. https://www.recode.net/2017/5/30/15693660/reid-hoffman-linkedin-greylock-partner-political-problem-investment-code-2017.

40. York, Byron. "In Politics Fight, Breitbart Knew Culture Is Key." Washington Examiner. March 01, 2012. Accessed August 08, 2018. https://www.washingtonexaminer.com/in-politics-fight-breitbart-knew-culture-is-key/article/1154466.

CHAPTER 7—DUMB CONCLUSION

1. Ingram, Emily. "Most Millennials Use Adderall Without A Prescription Or ADD." Elite Daily. December 13, 216. https://www.elitedaily.com/life/add-for-all-millennials-adderall-drug-ignored-consequences/1714144